Drop by companyscoming.com

Who We Are | Browse Cookbooks | Cooking Tonight? | Home

everyday ingredients

feature recipes

- **feature recipes** — Cooking tonight? Check out this month's **feature recipes**—absolutely FREE!

- **tips and tricks** — Looking for some great kitchen helpers? **tips and tricks** is here to save the day!

- **table talk** — In search of answers to cooking or household questions? Do you have answers you'd like to share? Join the fun with **table talk**, our on-line question and answer bulletin board. Our **table talk chat room** connects you with cooks from around the world. Great for swapping recipes too!

- **cooking links** — Other interesting and informative web-sites are just a click away with **cooking links**.

- **experts on-line** — Consult **experts on-line** for Jean Paré's time-saving tips and advice.

- **keyword search** — Find cookbooks by title, description or food category using **keyword search**.

- **e-mail us** — We want to hear from you—**e-mail us** lets you offer suggestions for upcoming titles, or share your favorite recipes.

Company's Coming **COOKBOOKS**

everyday recipes trusted by millions

Company's Coming Cookbooks

Original Series

- 150 Delicious Squares
- Appetizers
- Barbecues
- Breads
- Breakfasts & Brunches
- Cakes
- Casseroles
- Chicken, Etc.
- Cookies
- Cooking for Two
- Desserts
- Dinners of the World
- Fish & Seafood
- Holiday Entertaining
- Kids Cooking
- Light Casseroles
- Light Recipes
- Lunches
- Main Courses
- Make-Ahead Meals
- Meatless Cooking
- Microwave Cooking
- Muffins & More
- One-Dish Meals
- Pasta
- Pies
- Pizza!
- Preserves
- Salads
- Slow Cooker Recipes
- Soups & Sandwiches
- Starters
- Stir-Fry
- The Potato Book NEW (Nov/00)
- Vegetables

Greatest Hits Series

- Biscuits, Muffins & Loaves
- Dips, Spreads & Dressings
- Sandwiches & Wraps
- Soups & Salads

Lifestyle Series

- Grilling
- Low-Fat Cooking
- Low-Fat Pasta

Special Occasion Series

- Chocolate Everything NEW (Oct/00)
- Easy Entertaining

Other

- Beef Today!

Table of Contents

The Company's Coming Story . . 6

Foreword. 7

Guide to Potatoes 8

Getting Started 9

Cooking Basics. 10

Appetizers 11

Breads. 19

Soups 29

Salads 37

Main Dishes. 43

Side Dishes 61

Desserts. 139

Measurement Tables 151

Index. 152

Photo Index. 155

Tip Index. 156

Feature Recipe. 157

Mail Order Form 159

The Company's Coming Story

Jean Paré grew up understanding that the combination of family, friends and home cooking is the essence of a good life. From her mother she learned to appreciate good cooking, while her father praised even her earliest attempts. When she left home she took with her many acquired family recipes, a love of cooking and an intriguing desire to read recipe books like novels!

"never share a recipe you wouldn't use yourself"

In 1963, when her four children had all reached school age, Jean volunteered to cater the 50th anniversary of the Vermilion School of Agriculture, now Lakeland College. Working out of her home, Jean prepared a dinner for over 1000 people which launched a flourishing catering operation that continued for over eighteen years. During that time she was provided with countless opportunities to test new ideas with immediate feedback—resulting in empty plates and contented customers! Whether preparing cocktail sandwiches for a house party or serving a hot meal for 1500 people, Jean Paré earned a reputation for good food, courteous service and reasonable prices.

"Why don't you write a cookbook?" Time and again, as requests for her recipes mounted, Jean was asked that question. Jean's response was to team up with her son, Grant Lovig, in the fall of 1980 to form Company's Coming Publishing Limited. April 14, 1981, marked the debut of "150 DELICIOUS SQUARES", the first Company's Coming cookbook in what soon would become Canada's most popular cookbook series.

Jean Paré's operation has grown steadily from the early days of working out of a spare bedroom in her home. Full-time staff includes marketing personnel located in major cities across Canada. Home Office is based in Edmonton, Alberta in a modern building constructed specially for the company.

Today the company distributes throughout Canada and the United States in addition to numerous overseas markets, all under the guidance of Jean's daughter, Gail Lovig. Best-sellers many times over, Company's Coming cookbooks are published in English and French, plus a Spanish-language edition is available in Mexico. Familiar and trusted in home kitchens the world over, Company's Coming cookbooks are offered in a variety of formats, including the original softcover series.

Jean Paré's approach to cooking has always called for quick and easy recipes using everyday ingredients. Even when traveling, she is constantly on the lookout for new ideas to share with her readers. At home, she can usually be found researching and writing recipes, or working in the company's test kitchen. Jean continues to gain new supporters by adhering to what she calls "the golden rule of cooking": never share a recipe you wouldn't use yourself. It's an approach that works— *millions of times over!*

Foreword

Why a book devoted to potatoes? The potato is humble when considering its inexpensive production costs, but exalted in cooking circles around the world for its versatility. This earthy tuber can be simply prepared for a weekday supper or elegantly dressed up to grace the finest tables. Whether steamed, boiled, mashed, creamed, fried or baked, *The Potato Book* contains more than 150 kitchen-tested recipes for this nearly perfect food, ranging from appetizers to soups, and main courses to side dishes. You'll even find a section on desserts using potatoes!

First grown in South America several thousand years ago, this root vegetable traveled to Europe and North America with explorers in the late 1500s. Marie Antoinette made a fashion statement by wearing potato blossoms in her hair. Soon the potato became such a faithful standby of the poor that a crop failure, caused by a fungus in Ireland, led to the Great Potato Famine in the 1840s.

Potatoes have grown in popularity in North America over the past few decades, and have always been very popular with my family.

My children loved it when I would serve them mashed potatoes with a gravy-filled well in the center. Often as a grown-up, my daughter asks for such a well on family occasions, then shows her brothers, telling them that I like her best and that she's my favorite!

Potatoes, spuds or taters — whatever you choose to call them — are always a welcome addition to any meal. One medium potato contains about 100 calories and is 99.99 percent fat-free, so it is always a great choice for a healthy eating plan. Impress your family and friends with the many different ways you can prepare this seemingly ordinary vegetable. Think of it as a blank canvas on which to paint a masterpiece!

Jean Paré

Each recipe has been analyzed using the most up-to-date version of the Canadian Nutrient File from Health Canada, which is based upon the United States Department of Agriculture (USDA) Nutrient Data Base.

Margaret Ng, B.Sc. (Hon), M.A.
Registered Dietitian

guide to buying & cooking

WAXY (WET)		
Name	**Best used for**	**Characteristics**
Chieftan, Desiree, Kennebec, Norland, Red Pontiac, Sangre	boiling, roasting	▼ Most new or red potatoes ▼ Skin is thin ▼ Texture is creamy, firm ▼ Lower starch content ▼ Boils well, retains shape, even when cooked a few minutes too long

BAKING (DRY)		
Name	**Best used for**	**Characteristics**
Baker, Century Russet, Goldrush, Russet Burbank, Russet Norkotah, Shepody	baking, frying, mashing	▼ Old potatoes, left in ground longer or stored after harvesting ▼ Skin is thick, rough ▼ Shape is oblong ▼ Texture is dry ▼ Higher starch content ▼ Cooking time is faster than new potatoes; tends to crumble if overboiled

ALL-PURPOSE		
Name	**Best used for**	**Characteristics**
Bintje, Irish Cobbler, Katahdin, White Rose, Yukon Gold	baking, boiling, frying, mashing, roasting	▼ Red or tan skin (may also be blue or purple) ▼ Shape is oblong or round ▼ Flesh is white or yellow (or blue or purple) ▼ Yellow-fleshed varieties have rich flavor

SWEET POTATOES *		
Name	**Best used for**	**Characteristics**
Sweet potatoes	Interchangeable with regular potatoes in any recipe	▼ Skin is white to orange ▼ Shape is oblong and irregular ▼ Flesh is white to orange ▼ Texture ranges from dry to wet ▼ High in vitamins A and C, contain various minerals ▼ Often confused with yams and may be sold and labeled as such

Yams *		
Name	**Best used for**	**Characteristics**
Yams	Interchangeable with sweet potatoes in any recipe	▼ Skin is white to pink or dark brown ▼ Shape is round or oblong and irregular ▼ Flesh is white to yellow, pink to brownish pink ▼ Texture varies from dry to wet ▼ High in potassium and contain vitamins C and B6, thiamine, folic acid, magnesium, phosphorous and copper ▼ Not as sweet as sweet potatoes

* Store the same as potatoes, and use within a week of purchase. However, sweet potatoes and yams may last up to 4 weeks in a cool, dry location.

BUYING

Although we specify which type of potato to use in some of the recipes in *The Potato Book*, they are usually interchangeable. Grocery signs often explain the best uses for certain varieties.

▼ If you don't know what kind of potatoes you have, rub the skin. Waxy potatoes have thin, papery jackets that shred off like tissue.

▼ Choose potatoes that feel heavy and hard, without black or green spots, bruises, decay or sprouts.

▼ Avoid potatoes with green skin, since they've been exposed to light while growing or during storage. They may contain an alkaloid substance called solanine in the flesh near the peel, which makes them bitter tasting and potentially toxic if eaten in large quantities. Peeling and cooking in water reduces solanine levels.

▼ Soft or sprouted potatoes have lost almost all their nutrients, but are still edible.

STORAGE

Store potatoes loose, or in a paper bag, but not in the refrigerator, as the starches will convert to sugar. Store for months in a cold room at 45 to 50°F (7 to 10°C) in bulk. Avoid storing next to strong-smelling foods such as onions. If you lack a cold room, buy just enough potatoes to use within a few days and store in a dark cupboard. Warmth causes sprouts, damp causes rot, and light increases solanine levels. (See Buying, above.)

Cooked potatoes and sweet potatoes keep for up to six days in the refrigerator. Cooked mashed potatoes or stuffed potatoes can be frozen for up to two or three months. Don't freeze raw potatoes as they will go soft and unpalatable.

TO PEEL OR NOT TO PEEL

Although many recipes in *The Potato Book* call for peeled potatoes, discarding the skin is a matter of preference in most cases. Potatoes can be scrubbed clean and cooked with the peel on, then thinly peeled to retain flavor, fiber and nutrients. If you choose to peel before cooking, take off only a thin layer, since thick peeling is wasteful and results in valuable nutrients being lost. Cut out the eyes for esthetics but this step is essential if there are sprouts, since solanine levels are high there. (See Buying, above.)

SIZES AND EQUIVALENTS

Small potato: 5-6 oz. (140-170 g)
Medium potato: 7-8 oz. (200-225 g)
Large potato: 9-10 oz. (255-285 g)
1 pound (454 g): approximately 3 small, 2 medium, 1½ large
1 pound (454 g) thinly peeled potatoes = 2 cups (500 mL) mashed potatoes.

COOKING

Baked: Wash skin of baking potato well and pierce in several places with fork. Bake, without wrapping or greasing, until soft when squeezed or fork slides in easily. Wrapping in foil produces a steamed potato with pasty texture instead of dry and fluffy, but they can be foil-wrapped when done to retain the heat until served.

Bake in: 375°F (190°C) oven for 75 minutes.
400°F (205°C) oven for 70 minutes.
450°F (230°C) oven for 45 minutes.

Count on 1 medium potato (see above) per person. To be a connoisseur, poke an 'x' on the top of the baked potato with a fork, then press ends of potato together to pop the 'x.'

Mashed: Boil quartered potatoes until tender in water in a covered saucepan. Some recipes in *The Potato Book* call for salt in the cooking water, but otherwise it is optional. Drain and dry potatoes in the pot by shaking over low heat. Mash well with a hand masher, ricer or food mill. You may also use an electric beater, as long as you don't overbeat since this may result in a gluey texture. For *The Potato Book*, when a recipe calls for mashed potatoes, this is the method to use, without any other ingredients. If a recipe calls for leftover mashed potatoes it includes potato water or milk and margarine you used before.

▼ Cook potatoes in just a little water. The more liquid drained after cooking, the more nutrients that are lost. Use the cooking water afterwards for gravy, bread making or soup.

French-fried: See page 134.

Grilled: Cut potatoes into thick slices or wedges. Dry cut edges and brush with cooking oil or margarine. Cook on medium-hot grill until golden. Turn once.

Microwave: Prick potato all over with fork, wrap in paper towel and microwave on high (100%) for 4 to 6 minutes, turning halfway through cooking. If baking more than one at a time, increase cooking time.

Roasted: See page 67.

Veggie Fritters

Good vegetable flavor in a crispy coating. Vegetable color shows through the coating, so use a variety of vegetables for a nice presentation. These freeze well.

Potatoes (about 1 medium), peeled and cut up	½ lb.	225 g
Water		
Cauliflower (or carrot or broccoli), cut up (see Note)	½ lb.	225 g
Water		
Large egg, fork-beaten	1	1
Grated Parmesan cheese	2 tbsp.	30 mL
Salt	¼ tsp.	1 mL
Pepper	⅛ tsp.	0.5 mL
Large egg, fork-beaten	1	1
Cold water	2 tbsp.	30 mL
Fine dry bread crumbs	**¾ cup**	**175 mL**
Cooking oil, for deep-frying		

Cook potato in water in medium saucepan until tender. Drain. Mash.

Cook cauliflower in water in small saucepan until tender. Drain well. Add to potato. Mash.

Add first egg, cheese, salt and pepper. Mix well. Mixture will be soft. Chill for 1 hour.

Beat second egg and third amount of water in small bowl.

Drop vegetable mixture by ½ tablespoonfuls (7 mL) into egg mixture. Transfer to crumb mixture on tines of fork. Coat with crumbs. Shape into small balls.

Deep-fry, a few at a time, in 375°F (190°C) cooking oil for 1½ to 2 minutes until golden brown. Remove with slotted spoon to paper towels to drain. Makes about 45 fritters.

1 fritter: 23 Calories; 1 g Total Fat; 38 mg Sodium; 1 g Protein; 3 g Carbohydrate; trace Dietary Fiber

Note: Or use 3 oz., 85 g (¼ cup, 60 mL) of each vegetable, cooked separately.

To Make Ahead: Prepare and freeze for up to 3 months. To reheat from frozen state, place fritters on baking sheet in 400°F (205°C) oven for 10 to 15 minutes until hot.

Sweet Potato Balls

Deep-fried crispiness in these attractive tidbits makes them a great appetizer.

Sweet potatoes, peeled and cut up	1 lb.	454 g
Water		
All-purpose flour	⅓ cup	75 mL
Cornstarch	2 tbsp.	30 mL
Brown sugar, packed	2 tbsp.	30 mL
Salt, just a pinch		
Cooking oil, for deep-frying		

Cook sweet potato in water in medium saucepan until tender. Drain. Mash.

Stir flour, cornstarch, sugar and salt well in small bowl. Add to potato. Mash well. Shape into 1½ inch (3.8 cm) balls.

Deep-fry, a few at a time, in 375°F (190°C) cooking oil for about 5 minutes until browned. Remove with slotted spoon to paper towels to drain. Makes 24 balls.

1 ball: 54 Calories; 1.3 g Total Fat; 4 mg Sodium; 1 g Protein; 10 g Carbohydrate; 1 g Dietary Fiber

Pictured on page 35.

Vegetable Squares

Pretty finger food, hot or cold. A dot of sour cream and a tiny piece of fresh dill are all that's needed to dress up squares for serving.

Frozen shredded hash brown potatoes	3 cups	750 mL
Grated carrot	1 cup	250 mL
Minced onion flakes	1 tbsp.	15 mL
All-purpose flour	¼ cup	60 mL
Large eggs, fork-beaten	3	3
Lemon juice	2 tbsp.	30 mL
Cooking oil	2 tbsp.	30 mL
Dill weed	1 tsp.	5 mL
Garlic powder (optional)	⅛ tsp.	0.5 mL
Salt	1 tsp.	5 mL
Pepper	⅛ tsp.	0.5 mL

(continued on next page)

Mix all 11 ingredients in large bowl. Turn into greased 9 × 9 inch (22 × 22 cm) pan. Bake in 375°F (190°C) oven for about 40 minutes until set and browned. Cuts into 36 squares.

1 square: 33 Calories; 1.2 g Total Fat; 85 mg Sodium; 1 g Protein; 5 g Carbohydrate; 1 g Dietary Fiber

To Make Ahead: Bake squares and cool. Chill. To serve, microwave on high (100%) for 1 to 2 minutes, or reheat in 350°F (175°C) oven for 15 minutes.

Potato Appetizer Puffs

Good spicy flavor. Can be made ahead and reheated to serve.

Large eggs	2	2
Onion powder	¼ tsp.	1 mL
Dry mustard	¼ tsp.	1 mL
Cayenne pepper	⅛-¼ tsp.	0.5-1 mL
Salt	½ tsp.	2 mL
Pepper	⅛ tsp.	0.5 mL
Mashed potatoes	2 cups	500 mL
Fine dry bread crumbs	½ cup	125 mL
Powdered Cheddar cheese product	⅓ cup	75 mL
COATING		
Fine dry bread crumbs	2 tbsp.	30 mL
Powdered Cheddar cheese product	2 tbsp.	30 mL
Chili powder	½-1 tsp.	2-5 mL
Cooking oil, for deep-frying		

Beat first 6 ingredients in medium bowl until smooth.

Mix in potato, bread crumbs and cheese product. Shape into 1 inch (2.5 cm) balls.

Coating: Mix all 3 ingredients in small dish. Coat balls well.

Deep-fry in 375°F (190°C) cooking oil for 3 to 4 minutes until golden brown. Remove with slotted spoon to paper towels to drain. Makes 48 puffs.

1 puff: 29 Calories; 1.5 g Total Fat; 50 mg Sodium; 1 g Protein; 3 g Carbohydrate; trace Dietary Fiber

Sesame Sticks

Buttery, nutty flavor in the crispy exterior. Great as a dipper in your favorite sauce or as an accompaniment to soup.

Mashed potatoes	1 cup	250 mL
Margarine (or butter), softened	½ cup	125 mL
Seasoned salt	¼ tsp.	1 mL
All-purpose flour	1 cup	250 mL
Large egg, fork-beaten	1	1
Water	1 tbsp.	15 mL
Salt	½ tsp.	2 mL
Toasted sesame seeds	4 tsp.	20 mL

Mix potato, margarine and seasoned salt in medium bowl.

Add flour. Mix well. Chill for several hours or overnight for ease of handling. Roll ¼ inch (6 mm) thick.

Mix egg and water in cup. Brush over top.

Sprinkle with salt and sesame seeds. Cut into 4 inch (10 cm) strips about ½ inch (12 mm) wide. Transfer carefully to greased baking sheet with lifter. Bake in 400°F (205°C) oven for 20 minutes until golden brown and crisp. Makes 34 sticks.

2 sticks: 100 Calories; 6.5 g Total Fat; 173 mg Sodium; 2 g Protein; 9 g Carbohydrate; 1 g Dietary Fiber

Pictured on page 143 and back cover.

Dilly Potato Tots

Crispy on the outside and tender inside with a dominant dill presence.

Package of frozen potato tots or gems	1¾ lbs.	790 g
Envelope of dill dip mix (or sauce), 1 oz. (28 g)	2 tbsp.	30 mL

Spread potato tots on ungreased baking sheet. Sprinkle with dill dip mix. Bake in 450°F (230°C) oven for 20 minutes, turning at half-time. Makes 7 cups (1.75 L).

1 serving: 247 Calories; 11.6 g Total Fat; 1086 mg Sodium; 4 g Protein; 35 g Carbohydrate; 3 g Dietary Fiber

Samosas

Potatoes in a potato crust with all those exotic East Indian flavors. Takes a little longer to prepare but the final result is well worth it.

CRUST		
Mashed baking potatoes (see Note)	2 cups	500 mL
Large egg, fork-beaten	1	1
All-purpose flour	1¼ cups	300 mL
Salt	½ tsp.	2 mL
FILLING		
Diced cooked potato	1½ cups	375 mL
Frozen peas, thawed	½ cup	125 mL
Ground cumin	¾ tsp.	4 mL
Cayenne pepper (Indian chili powder)	¼ tsp.	1 mL
Turmeric	¼ tsp.	1 mL
Ground coriander	½ tsp.	2 mL
Salt	½ tsp.	2 mL
Large egg, fork-beaten	1	1

Crust: Mix all 4 ingredients in medium bowl to form soft ball of dough. Roll ½ of dough out on well-floured surface in 11 × 14 inch (28 × 35 cm) rectangle. Cut into 3½ inch (9 cm) squares.

Filling: Mix first 7 ingredients in medium bowl. Spoon rounded tablespoonfuls (15 mL) onto one side of center in each square. Dampen two adjoining sides. Fold over diagonally. Seal edges with floured fork.

Brush tops with egg. Place on greased baking sheet. Bake in 400°F (205°C) oven for 14 to 15 minutes. Repeat with remaining dough and filling. Makes 24 samosas.

1 samosa: 59 Calories; 0.6 g Total Fat; 124 mg Sodium; 2 g Protein; 12 g Carbohydrate; 1 g Dietary Fiber

Note: Baking potatoes are used for the crust due to their dry texture. Use for filling as well, if desired.

Variation: Omit brushing with egg. Deep-fry, a few at a time, in 375°F (190°C) cooking oil for 3½ to 4 minutes until golden brown. Remove with slotted spoon to paper towels to drain.

Cheesy Potato Skins

Always a popular appetizer with crispy texture!

Cooking oil	1 tsp.	5 mL
Unpeeled medium potatoes	4	4
Grated light sharp Cheddar cheese	1 cup	250 mL
Chopped chives (or green onion tops)	1 tbsp.	15 mL
Sour cream	½ cup	125 mL
Salsa	½ cup	125 mL

Rub few drops of cooking oil over surface of each potato. Set potatoes on oven rack. Bake in 425°F (220°C) oven for about 40 minutes until tender. Cool.

Cut each potato in half lengthwise. Remove pulp, leaving skins ¼ inch (6 mm) thick. Cut each half into 4 wedges. Spray each wedge on the skin side with no-stick cooking spray (or brush with cooking oil). Arrange, skin side down, on greased baking sheet. Sprinkle with cheese and chives. Bake in 425°F (220°C) oven for 10 to 13 minutes until cheese is melted and heated through.

Serve with sour cream and salsa for dipping. Makes 32 potato skins.

2 potato skins: 47 Calories; 2.9 g Total Fat; 174 mg Sodium; 3 g Protein; 3 g Carbohydrate; trace Dietary Fiber

1. Brown Grain Bread, page 24
2. Potato Broccoli Soup, page 29
3. Savory Potato Soup, page 30

Props Courtesy Of: Stokes

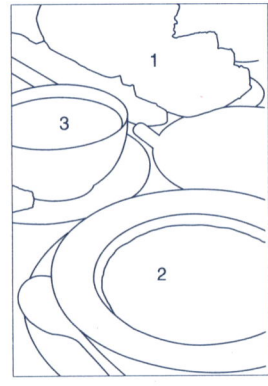

Potato Wheat Biscuits

Cheesy and wholesome. Good on their own or with chili or soup.

All-purpose flour	1 cup	250 mL
Whole wheat flour	¾ cup	175 mL
Grated light sharp Cheddar cheese	½ cup	125 mL
Grated light Parmesan cheese	2 tbsp.	30 mL
Baking powder	1 tbsp.	15 mL
Salt	½ tsp.	2 mL
Milk	⅔ cup	150 mL
Cooking oil	3 tbsp.	50 mL
Mashed potatoes	1 cup	250 mL
Grated light sharp Cheddar cheese	¼ cup	60 mL

Stir first 6 ingredients together in large bowl. Make a well.

Mix milk, cooking oil and potato in medium bowl until smooth. Pour into well. Stir to form soft ball. Turn out and knead 6 to 8 times on lightly floured surface. Divide into 12 equal portions. Shape into round balls. Place in greased 9 inch (22 cm) round cake pan. Bake in 425°F (220°C) oven for 15 minutes.

Sprinkle with second amount of Cheddar cheese. Bake for about 5 minutes until browned. Makes 12 biscuits.

1 biscuit: 147 Calories; 5.5 g Total Fat; 193 mg Sodium; 5 g Protein; 19 g Carbohydrate; 2 g Dietary Fiber

Pictured on page 143 and back cover.

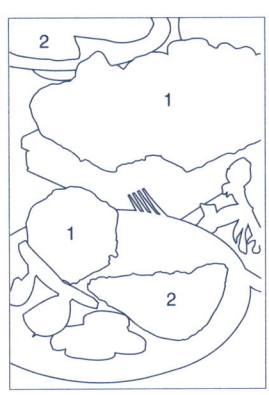

1. Cinnamon Buns, page 22
2. Spanish Omelet, page 76

Props Courtesy Of: The Bay

Quickest Potato Biscuits

Don't know what to do with the leftover potatoes? Make biscuits!

Mashed potatoes	½ cup	125 mL
Milk	½ cup	125 mL
Biscuit mix	2 cups	500 mL

Beat potato and milk in medium bowl until smooth.

Stir in biscuit mix to form soft ball. Turn out and knead 8 to 10 times on lightly floured surface. Roll or pat ¾ inch (2 cm) thick. Cut into 2 inch (5 cm) circles with cookie cutter. Arrange on greased baking sheet. Bake in 425°F (220°C) oven for 13 to 15 minutes until risen and golden brown. Makes 16 biscuits.

1 biscuit: 81 Calories; 2.2 g Total Fat; 224 mg Sodium; 2 g Protein; 13 g Carbohydrate; trace Dietary Fiber

Potato Biscuits

A heavier biscuit that is delicious with soup.

All-purpose flour	1¾ cups	425 mL
Baking powder	1 tbsp.	15 mL
Granulated sugar	2 tsp.	10 mL
Salt	¾ tsp.	4 mL
Hard margarine (or butter)	¼ cup	60 mL
Mashed potatoes	¾ cup	175 mL
Milk	½ cup	125 mL

Stir flour, baking powder, sugar and salt in large bowl. Cut in margarine until crumbly. Make a well.

Mix potato and milk in medium bowl until smooth. Pour into well. Mix to form soft ball. Turn out and knead 8 to 10 times on lightly floured surface. Pat or roll ¾ inch (2 cm) thick. Cut into circles with 2 inch (5 cm) cookie cutter. Arrange on greased baking sheet. Bake in 425°F (220°C) oven for 13 to 15 minutes until risen and golden brown. Makes 16 biscuits.

1 biscuit: 96 Calories; 3.3 g Total Fat; 67 mg Sodium; 2 g Protein; 14 g Carbohydrate; 1 g Dietary Fiber

Currant Scones

These have a sugar sparkle on top.

All-purpose flour	2 cups	500 mL
Granulated sugar	2 tbsp.	30 mL
Baking powder	4 tsp.	20 mL
Cream of tartar	½ tsp.	2 mL
Salt	½ tsp.	2 mL
Ground nutmeg	¼ tsp.	1 mL
Hard margarine (or butter)	6 tbsp.	100 mL
Large egg, fork-beaten	1	1
Mashed potatoes	¾ cup	175 mL
Milk	½ cup	125 mL
Currants	½ cup	125 mL
Granulated sugar	1 tbsp.	15 mL

Stir first 6 ingredients in large bowl. Cut in margarine until crumbly. Make a well.

Mix egg, potato and milk in medium bowl. Pour into well.

Add currants to potato mixture. Mix to form soft ball. Turn out and knead 6 times on lightly floured surface. Roll or pat into ¾ inch (2 cm) thick circle. Cut into 2 inch (5 cm) rounds. Arrange on greased baking sheet.

Sprinkle each with ⅛ tsp. (0.5 mL) sugar. Bake in 425°F (220°C) oven for 15 to 20 minutes until golden brown. Makes 24 scones.

1 scone: 89 Calories; 3.7 g Total Fat; 111 mg Sodium; 2 g Protein; 12 g Carbohydrate; 1 g Dietary Fiber

 *To use leftover cooked potatoes in bread recipes, substitute milk and/or water for the reserved potato liquid.*

Cinnamon Buns

These have a light texture and rise beautifully into delicious, high buns.

Hot potato water (or hot water)	2½ cups	625 mL
Mashed potatoes	1 cup	250 mL
Margarine (or butter)	½ cup	125 mL
Large eggs	2	2
Granulated sugar	½ cup	125 mL
Salt	1½ tsp.	7 mL
All-purpose flour	3½ cups	875 mL
Instant yeast (or 2 envelopes, ¼ oz., 8 g, each)	5 tsp.	25 mL
All-purpose flour, approximately	4 cups	1 L
FILLING		
Margarine (or butter), softened	⅔ cup	150 mL
Ground cinnamon	2 tbsp.	30 mL
Brown sugar, packed	1 cup	250 mL
ICING		
Icing (confectioner's) sugar	1½ cups	375 mL
Margarine (or butter), softened	3 tbsp.	50 mL
Vanilla	½ tsp.	2 mL
Milk (or water)	3 tbsp.	50 mL

Beat first 6 ingredients in large bowl until margarine is melted.

Add first amount of flour and yeast. Beat for about 2 minutes.

Work in enough of second amount of flour until dough pulls away from sides of bowl. Turn out and knead 8 to 10 minutes on floured surface until smooth and elastic. Divide into 3 equal portions. Roll 1 portion at a time into 9 × 12 inch (22 × 30 cm) rectangle.

Filling: Spread each rectangle with ⅓ of margarine.

Mix cinnamon and brown sugar in small bowl. Sprinkle ⅓ evenly over each rectangle. Roll up each from long side. Cut into twelve 1 inch (2.5 cm) slices. Arrange in 2 greased 9 × 13 inch (22 × 33 cm) pans. Cover with tea towels. Let stand in oven with light on and door closed for about 1 hour until doubled in size. Bake one pan at a time in 375°F (190°C) oven for about 20 minutes until browned. Turn out on racks to cool slightly. Turn right side up to ice.

(continued on next page)

Icing: Beat all 4 ingredients in small bowl until smooth, adding more icing sugar or milk as necessary to make a thin glaze. Spoon or drizzle over warm buns. Makes 3 dozen buns.

1 iced bun: 233 Calories; 7.9 g Total Fat; 206 mg Sodium; 4 g Protein; 37 g Carbohydrate; 1 g Dietary Fiber

Pictured on page 18.

Potato Hotcakes

These wee cakes are delicious with syrup. Try the various suggestions below for lunch with a dab of sour cream.

Mashed potatoes	1 cup	250 mL
Large egg, fork-beaten	1	1
Salt	½ tsp.	2 mL
Granulated sugar	2 tsp.	10 mL
Milk	1 cup	250 mL
Hard margarine (or butter), melted	1 tbsp.	15 mL
All-purpose flour	1 cup	250 mL
Baking powder	1 tbsp.	15 mL

Stir potato and egg in medium bowl. Add salt, sugar, milk and margarine. Mix.

Stir in flour and baking powder, adding a bit more milk to make spoonable, but barely pourable, batter. Grease frying pan with cooking spray for each batch. Heat pan. Drop batter by tablespoonful (15 mL) into pan. Brown both sides. Makes 34 small hotcakes.

2 hotcakes: 60 Calories; 1.2 g Total Fat; 103 mg Sodium; 2 g Protein; 10 g Carbohydrate; trace Dietary Fiber

CHEDDAR HOTCAKES: Add 1 cup (250 mL) grated sharp Cheddar with dry ingredients.

GREEN ONION HOTCAKES: Add ¼ cup (60 mL) finely chopped green onion with dry ingredients.

DELUXE CHEESE AND ONION HOTCAKES: Add 1 cup (250 mL) grated sharp Cheddar and ¼ cup (60 mL) finely chopped green onion with dry ingredients.

Paré Pointer

She knew she had found a lost ball. The boy across the street was still looking for it.

Brown Grain Bread

A slightly sweet taste from molasses makes these perfect to serve with baked beans or hearty soups.

All-purpose flour	1 cup	250 mL
Whole wheat flour	1 cup	250 mL
All-bran cereal	½ cup	125 mL
Rolled oats (not instant)	½ cup	125 mL
Granulated sugar	2 tbsp.	30 mL
Instant yeast (or ¼ oz., 8 g, envelope)	2½ tsp.	12 mL
Salt	2 tsp.	10 mL
Very warm water	2 cups	500 mL
Milk	¼ cup	60 mL
Fancy (mild) molasses	⅓ cup	75 mL
Hard margarine (or butter)	¼ cup	60 mL
Mashed potatoes	1 cup	250 mL
All-purpose flour, approximately	4½ cups	1.1 L
Hard margarine (or butter), softened	2 tsp.	10 mL

Measure first 7 ingredients into large bowl. Stir. Make a well. Pour potato mixture into well. Beat for 2 minutes.

Add water, milk, molasses, first amount of margarine and mashed potato. Heat and stir until very warm and margarine is melted. Pour into well. Beat for 2 minutes.

Work in enough of second amount of all-purpose flour until dough pulls away from sides of bowl. Turn out and knead for 8 to 10 minutes on floured surface until smooth and elastic. Place in greased large bowl, turning once to grease top. Cover with tea towel. Let stand in oven with light on and door closed for about 1¼ hours until doubled in bulk. Punch dough down. Divide in half. Shape into 2 loaves. Place in 2 greased 9 × 5 × 3 inch (22 × 12.5 × 7.5 cm) loaf pans. Cover with tea towel. Let stand in oven with light on and door closed for about 45 minutes until doubled in size. Bake in 375°F (190°C) oven for 35 to 40 minutes. Cover with brown paper or foil for last 10 minutes if tops brown too quickly. Turn out onto racks to cool.

Brush hot loaf tops with second amount of margarine. Makes 2 loaves, 12 slices each.

1 slice: 186 Calories; 3 g Total Fat; 271 mg Sodium; 5 g Protein; 36 g Carbohydrate; 2 g Dietary Fiber

Pictured on page 17.

Sweet Potato Loaf

This pleasant spice loaf is dense and moist.

Hard margarine (or butter), softened	½ cup	125 mL
Granulated sugar	¼ cup	60 mL
Brown sugar, packed	¼ cup	60 mL
Large eggs	2	2
Mashed sweet potatoes	1 cup	250 mL
Fancy (mild) molasses	¼ cup	60 mL
Vanilla	1 tsp.	5 mL
All-purpose flour	2 cups	500 mL
Baking powder	½ tsp.	2 mL
Baking soda	1 tsp.	5 mL
Salt	½ tsp.	2 mL
Ground cinnamon	¾ tsp.	4 mL
Ground nutmeg	½ tsp.	2 mL
Ground allspice	¼ tsp.	1 mL

Cream margarine and both sugars in large bowl. Beat in eggs, 1 at a time. Add sweet potato, molasses and vanilla. Mix.

Stir remaining 7 ingredients together in medium bowl. Add to potato mixture. Stir just to moisten. Turn into greased 9 × 5 × 3 inch (22 × 12.5 × 7.5 cm) loaf pan. Bake in 350°F (175°C) oven for 50 to 60 minutes. A wooden pick inserted in center should come out clean. Cuts into 16 slices.

1 slice: 189 Calories; 7 g Total Fat; 256 mg Sodium; 3 g Protein; 29 g Carbohydrate; 1 g Dietary Fiber

Variation: Add ½ cup (125 mL) raisins or chopped walnuts when adding spices.

Paré Pointer
The sign said, "No standing anytime," so he sat down on the curb.

Potato Bread

A nice textured bread.

Potatoes (about 1 large), peeled and cut up	¾ lb.	340 g
Water	2 cups	500 mL
Hard margarine (or butter)	6 tbsp.	100 mL
Reserved potato water, plus milk to make	2¼ cups	550 mL
Granulated sugar	3 tbsp.	50 mL
Salt	2 tsp.	10 mL
All-purpose flour	3 cups	750 mL
Instant yeast (or ¼ oz., 8 g, envelope)	2½ tsp.	12 mL
All-purpose flour, approximately	5 cups	1.25 L
Hard margarine (or butter), softened	2 tsp.	10 mL

Cook potato in water in medium saucepan until tender. Drain and reserve potato water. Mash potato in saucepan.

Add first amount of margarine, reserved potato water with milk, sugar and salt. Heat and stir until margarine is melted. Turn into large bowl. Cool slightly. Mixture should still be quite hot, not lukewarm.

Add first amount of flour and yeast. Beat for 2 minutes.

Work in enough of the second amount of flour until dough pulls away from sides of bowl. Turn out and knead on floured surface for about 10 minutes until smooth and elastic. Place in large greased bowl, turning once to grease top. Cover with tea towel. Let stand in oven with light on and door closed for 1 hour until doubled in bulk. Punch dough down. Shape into 2 loaves. Place in 2 greased 9 × 5 × 3 inch (22 × 12.5 × 7.5 cm) loaf pans. Cover with tea towel. Let stand in oven with light on and door closed for 30 minutes until almost doubled in size. Bake in 375°F (190°C) oven for 30 minutes until golden brown. Turn out onto racks to cool.

Brush hot loaf tops with second amount of margarine. Makes 2 loaves, 12 slices each.

1 slice: 146 Calories; 3.6 g Total Fat; 267 mg Sodium; 3 g Protein; 25 g Carbohydrate; 1 g Dietary Fiber

Most types of cooked potatoes are great for reheating from frozen, such as mashed, baked, stuffed, patties and fries. The exceptions are those in soups or stews or raw potatoes which may crumble when thawed and reheated. Since it is the larger pieces that tend to go soppy, use grated raw potatoes to freeze in soups and stews.

Potato Buns

Pleasant, slightly sweet flavor in a chewy bun with substance!

Potatoes (about 1 medium), peeled and cut up	½ lb.	225 g
Water	2 cups	500 mL
Hard margarine (or butter)	½ cup	125 mL
Granulated sugar	½ cup	125 mL
Salt	1 tsp.	5 mL
All-purpose flour	2 cups	500 mL
Instant yeast (or ¼ oz., 8 g, envelope)	2½ tsp.	12 mL
Large egg, fork-beaten	1	1
All-purpose flour, approximately	4 cups	1 L

Cook potato in water in medium saucepan until tender. Drain, reserving 1⅓ cups (325 mL) potato water. Mash potato in saucepan.

Add reserved potato water, margarine, sugar and salt. Heat and stir until margarine is melted. Turn into large bowl. Cool slightly. Mixture should still be quite hot, not lukewarm.

Add first amount of flour, yeast and egg. Beat for 2 minutes.

Work in enough of second amount of flour until dough pulls away from sides of bowl and is smooth and elastic. Turn out and knead on floured surface for 5 minutes. Divide dough into 3 equal portions. Shape each portion into 12 balls. Arrange 1 inch (2.5 cm) apart in 2 greased 11 x 17 inch (28 x 43 cm) pans. Cover with tea towel. Let stand in oven with light on and door closed for about 1½ hours until almost doubled in size. Bake one pan at a time in 400°F (205°C) oven for 10 to 15 minutes until golden brown. Turn out onto racks to cool. Makes 3 dozen buns.

1 bun: 122 Calories; 3.1 g Total Fat; 110 mg Sodium; 3 g Protein; 21 g Carbohydrate; 1 g Dietary Fiber

Pictured on page 54.

POTATO TRAY BUNS: Arrange 18 balls of dough, touching each other, in each of 2 greased 9 x 13 inch (22 x 33 cm) pans. Rise and bake as above.

Paré Pointer
It has been rumored that witches will continue to fly on broomsticks because vacuum cords still aren't long enough.

Doughnuts

A sweet cake doughnut with a trace of nutmeg in the taste.

Mashed potatoes	½ cup	125 mL
Buttermilk (or reconstituted from powder)	¾ cup	175 mL
Large eggs	2	2
Granulated sugar	¾ cup	175 mL
Hard margarine (or butter), melted	¼ cup	60 mL
Vanilla	1 tsp.	5 mL
All-purpose flour	3⅞ cups	950 mL
Baking powder	1 tbsp.	15 mL
Baking soda	1 tsp.	5 mL
Ground nutmeg	½ tsp.	2 mL
Ground cinnamon	¼ tsp.	1 mL

Cooking oil, for deep-frying

Beat first 6 ingredients in large bowl.

Stir flour, baking powder, baking soda, nutmeg and cinnamon together in medium bowl. Add to potato mixture. Stir to moisten. Dough will be thick. Roll dough out on lightly floured surface scant ½ inch (12 mm) thick. Cut with doughnut cutter.

Deep-fry 2 or 3 doughnuts at a time in 375°F (190°C) cooking oil until golden brown on both sides. Remove with slotted spoon to paper towels to drain. Deep-fry "holes." Remove with slotted spoon to paper towels to drain. Makes 18 doughnuts and 18 "holes."

1 doughnut: 195 Calories; 7.6 g Total Fat; 130 mg Sodium; 4 g Protein; 28 g Carbohydrate; 1 g Dietary Fiber

SUGARED DOUGHNUTS: Pour ⅓ cup (75 mL) granulated sugar into plastic bag. Add 2 or 3 cooled doughnuts at a time. Shake to coat.

CINNAMON DOUGHNUTS: Pour ⅓ cup (75 mL) granulated sugar and rounded ¼ tsp. (1 mL) cinnamon in plastic bag. Add 2 or 3 cooled doughnuts at a time. Shake to coat.

Paré Pointer

To learn how to spell centimeter, Johnny was asked to write it in a sentence. He wrote, "A lady was coming to visit and I was sent-to-meet-her."

Potato Broccoli Soup

It's your choice: puréed smooth or left chunky. Garnish with a broccoli floret for a nice presentation.

Medium onions, chopped	2	2
Garlic clove, minced (or ¼ tsp., 1 mL, powder), optional	1	1
Margarine (or butter)	1 tbsp.	15 mL
Peeled diced potato	4 cups	1 L
Vegetable bouillon powder	2 tbsp.	30 mL
Diced broccoli	4 cups	1 L
Salt	1 tsp.	5 mL
Pepper	¼ tsp.	1 mL
Water	6 cups	1.5 L
Can of skim evaporated milk	13½ oz.	385 mL
Grated light sharp Cheddar cheese	½ cup	125 mL

Sauté onion and garlic in margarine in large saucepan or Dutch oven for about 10 minutes until soft and starting to turn golden.

Add next 6 ingredients. Bring to a boil. Cook until potatoes are tender. Do not drain.

Stir in milk. Remove some of the solids with slotted spoon to small bowl. Purée remainder. Add solids.

Sprinkle each serving with 1 tbsp. (15 mL) grated cheese. Makes 10¾ cups (2.7 L).

1 cup (250 mL): 129 Calories; 2.6 g Total Fat; 691 mg Sodium; 7 g Protein; 20 g Carbohydrate; 2 g Dietary Fiber

Pictured on page 17.

Paré Pointer
They tried the meatballs and found them guilty.

Vichyssoise

Pronounced vihsh-ee-SWAHZ. This classic soup must be served very cold.

Peeled, cubed potatoes	4 cups	1 L
Leeks (white part only), cut up	3	3
Medium onion, sliced	1	1
Parsley flakes	1 tsp.	5 mL
Salt	1 tsp.	5 mL
Pepper	¼ tsp.	1 mL
Ground nutmeg	⅛₆ tsp.	0.5 mL
Can of condensed chicken broth	10 oz.	284 mL
Water	1¾ cups	425 mL
Skim evaporated milk (or light cream)	⅔ cup	150 mL
Milk	1 cup	250 mL

Chopped chives, for garnish

Combine first 9 ingredients in large saucepan. Cook until vegetables are tender. Do not drain. Purée in blender. Pour into large bowl.

Stir in both milks. Cover. Chill for several hours.

Sprinkle chives on top. Makes 8 cups (2 L).

1 cup (250 mL): 121 Calories; 1 g Total Fat; 630 mg Sodium; 6 g Protein; 22 g Carbohydrate; 2 g Dietary Fiber

Savory Potato Soup

Such a pretty coral color. Pleasing flavor. Serve with a garnish of toasted croutons.

Peeled, cubed potatoes	2½ cups	625 mL
Cubed yellow turnip (rutabaga)	1½ cups	375 mL
Cubed carrot	1 cup	250 mL
Chopped onion	1 cup	250 mL
Water	3 cups	750 mL
Salt	1½ tsp.	7 mL
Pepper	⅛ tsp.	0.5 mL
Milk	4 cups	1 L

(continued on next page)

Cook first 7 ingredients in large saucepan or Dutch oven for about 20 minutes until tender. Purée vegetables and liquid in 2 or 3 batches in blender. Return to saucepan.

Add milk. Heat slowly, stirring often. Makes 9 cups (2.25 L).

1 cup (250 mL): 105 Calories; 1.4 g Total Fat; 463 mg Sodium; 5 g Protein; 19 g Carbohydrate; 2 g Dietary Fiber

Pictured on page 17.

Celery Cream Soup

A thick and creamy soup with a fresh celery taste.

Chopped celery (about 16 ribs)	8 cups	2 L
Medium onion, cut up	1	1
Water	3 cups	750 mL
Parsley flakes	1 tsp.	5 mL
Bay leaf	1	1
Dried thyme	¼ tsp.	1 mL
Chicken bouillon powder	1 tbsp.	15 mL
Salt	1 tsp.	5 mL
Pepper, sprinkle		
Mashed potatoes	1 cup	250 mL
Milk	2 cups	500 mL
Skim evaporated milk	⅔ cup	150 mL

Combine first 9 ingredients in large saucepan. Cook until vegetables are tender. Do not drain. Discard bay leaf. Purée with liquid in 2 or 3 batches in blender. Return to saucepan.

Add potato and both milks. Heat, stirring often, until bubbly hot. Makes 8 cups (2 L).

1 cup (250 mL): 99 Calories; 1.1 g Total Fat; 754 mg Sodium; 6 g Protein; 17 g Carbohydrate; 3 g Dietary Fiber

An extra mouth to feed? Not quite enough soup or chili? Microwave a potato, peel, dice and stir in to stretch that recipe.

Cullen Skink

From Scotland where smoked fish soup began. A good cold-day supper with a thick slice of bread. Traditionally served with pieces of butter melting on top or with swirls of whipping cream.

Finnan haddie (smoked haddock)	1 lb.	454 g
Medium onion, chopped	1	1
Water	3 cups	750 mL
Mashed potatoes	2½ cups	625 mL
Skim evaporated milk	⅔ cup	150 mL
Milk	1¾ cups	425 mL
Chopped fresh parsley (or 1 tsp., 5 mL, flakes)	1½ tbsp.	25 mL
Pepper	⅛ tsp.	0.5 mL

Cook fish and onion in water in large saucepan for 20 minutes. Do not drain. Remove fish. Remove bones, flaking flesh from skin. Return to saucepan.

Add remaining 5 ingredients. Bring to a boil, stirring frequently. Makes 8 cups (2 L).

1 cup (250 mL): 174 Calories; 1.3 g Total Fat; 492 mg Sodium; 19 g Protein; 21 g Carbohydrate; 1 g Dietary Fiber

Potato Sausage Soup

A hearty tummy warmer. Use stick pepperoni for more spice.

Peeled, cubed potatoes	3 cups	750 mL
Medium onion, chopped	1	1
Paprika	2 tsp.	10 mL
Ground marjoram	½ tsp.	2 mL
Salt	½ tsp.	2 mL
Pepper	¼ tsp.	1 mL
Garlic powder	¼ tsp.	1 mL
Beef bouillon powder	1 tbsp.	15 mL
Water	2 cups	500 mL
Diced summer sausage (or pepperoni)	½ cup	125 mL
Water	2 cups	500 mL
Light sour cream	¼ cup	60 mL

(continued on next page)

Cook first 9 ingredients in large saucepan for about 20 minutes until vegetables are tender. Do not drain. Mash well.

Add sausage and remaining water. Simmer for 5 minutes.

Serve with dollop of sour cream. Makes 5 cups (1.25 L).

1 cup (250 mL): 156 Calories; 7.9 g Total Fat; 944 mg Sodium; 6 g Protein; 16 g Carbohydrate; 2 g Dietary Fiber

Asparagus Chowder

Creamy and smooth describe this thick soup. Swirl with some whipping cream for an elegant first course when entertaining.

Peeled, cubed potatoes	2 cups	500 mL
Reserved asparagus liquid, plus water to make	2 cups	500 mL
Cans of asparagus spears (12 oz., 341 mL, each), drained and liquid reserved	2	2
Skim evaporated milk	⅔ cup	150 mL
Water	1 cup	250 mL
Onion powder	¼ tsp.	1 mL
Salt	½ tsp.	2 mL
Pepper	⅛-¼ tsp.	0.5-1 mL
Margarine (or butter)	1 tbsp.	15 mL
Granulated sugar	1 tbsp.	15 mL
Grated Havarti (or other) cheese, sprinkle, for garnish		
Grated nutmeg, light sprinkle, for garnish		
Fresh asparagus tips, steamed until tender, for garnish		

Cook potato in asparagus liquid in medium saucepan until tender. Do not drain. Turn into blender.

Add asparagus. Process until smooth. Return to saucepan.

Mix in next 7 ingredients. Simmer for 5 minutes, stirring often, to blend flavors.

Sprinkle with cheese and nutmeg. To serve, arrange asparagus tips over surface. Makes 4½ cups (1.1 L).

1 cup (250 mL): 143 Calories; 3.1 g Total Fat; 926 mg Sodium; 7 g Protein; 24 g Carbohydrate; 3 g Dietary Fiber

Pictured on page 143 and back cover.

Variation: To use fresh asparagus, cook 1½ lbs. (680 g) chopped asparagus in 2 cups (500 mL) water. Do not drain.

Mashed Potato Soup

A delicious, smooth soup. An ideal way to use leftover potatoes.

Water	3 cups	750 mL
Chicken bouillon cubes (⅕ oz., 5 g, each)	2	2
Finely chopped onion	⅓ cup	75 mL
Finely chopped celery	¼ cup	60 mL
Parsley flakes	1 tbsp.	15 mL
Salt	¾ tsp.	4 mL
Pepper (white is best)	⅛ tsp.	0.5 mL
Garlic powder (optional)	¹⁄₁₆ tsp.	0.5 mL
Milk	3 cups	750 mL
Mashed potatoes	4 cups	1 L

Heat water and bouillon cubes in large uncovered pot or Dutch oven until cubes are dissolved.

Add onion, celery, parsley, salt, pepper and garlic powder. Bring to a boil. Cover. Simmer for about 10 minutes until vegetables are tender.

Add milk and potato. Heat and stir to mix in potato. Whisk or use electric mixer to make smooth if desired. Reheat without boiling. Makes 8 cups (2 L).

1 cup (250 mL): 145 Calories; 1.2 g Total Fat; 667 mg Sodium; 5 g Protein; 29 g Carbohydrate; 2 g Dietary Fiber

1. Cranberry Sweet Potatoes, page 130
2. Sweet Potato Balls, page 12
3. Meaty Roulade, page 44

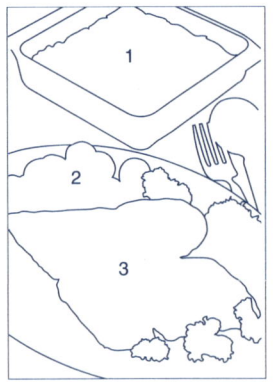

Southern Potato Salad

A different potato salad with zippy flavor and a snappy crunch.

White vinegar	2 tbsp.	30 mL
Granulated sugar	1 tbsp.	15 mL
Cooking oil	2 tbsp.	30 mL
Chili powder	1 tsp.	5 mL
Salt	¾ tsp.	4 mL
Pepper	¼ tsp.	1 mL
Peeled, cooked, diced waxy potatoes	4 cups	1 L
Chopped red onion	½ cup	125 mL
Chopped red pepper	⅓ cup	75 mL
Chopped chives	1 tbsp.	15 mL
Cooked frozen kernel (or canned, drained) corn	1 cup	250 mL

Measure first 6 ingredients into medium bowl. Stir well.

Add remaining 5 ingredients. Toss gently to coat well. Chill for 1 to 2 hours to blend flavors. Makes 5 cups (1.25 L).

1 cup (250 mL): 144 Calories; 4.6 g Total Fat; 399 mg Sodium; 2 g Protein; 25 g Carbohydrate; 2 g Dietary Fiber

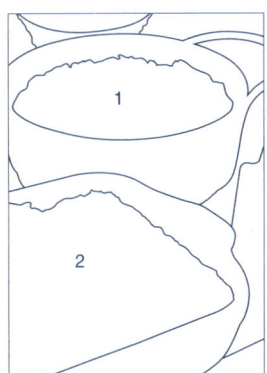

1. Apple Sweet Potato Bake, page 133
2. Dumpling Casserole, page 48

Props Courtesy Of: The Bay

Baked Potato Salad

Stuffed potato flavor in a casserole.

Waxy potatoes (about 5 medium), peeled and quartered	2½ lbs.	1.1 kg
Water		
Salt	½ tsp.	2 mL
Chopped red onion	⅔ cup	150 mL
Process cheese loaf (such as Velveeta)	4 oz.	113 g
Light salad dressing (or mayonnaise)	¾ cup	175 mL
Milk	3 tbsp.	50 mL
Salt	½ tsp.	2 mL
Pepper	¼ tsp.	1 mL
Bacon slices, diced	6	6

Cook potatoes in water and salt in large saucepan until tender but firm. Drain. Cool enough to handle. Cut into cubes. Place in large bowl.

Add next 6 ingredients. Toss gently to coat. Turn into greased 2 quart (2 L) casserole or 9 x 9 inch (22 x 22 cm) pan.

Sauté bacon until browned. Drain well on paper towel. Sprinkle bacon over salad. Bake in 350°F (175°C) oven for about 60 minutes until golden brown. Makes 7½ cups (1.9 L).

¾ cup (175 mL): 222 Calories; 11.9 g Total Fat; 659 mg Sodium; 6 g Protein; 23 g Carbohydrate; 1 g Dietary Fiber

Variation: Add ½ cup (125 mL) chopped green onion to potatoes before turning into baking dish.

 *To keep potatoes warm, put into 200°F (95°C) oven for a short time. Potato dishes may be reheated in 350°F (175°C) oven until hot.*

German Potato Salad

Served warm, this salad is scrumptious with lots of bacon and onion. Garnish with chopped green onion and carrot zest.

Waxy potatoes (about 4 medium), peeled and quartered	2 lbs.	900 g
Water		
Salt	¾ tsp.	4 mL
Pepper	⅛ tsp.	0.5 mL
Bacon slices, diced	6	6
Chopped onion	1 cup	250 mL
Granulated sugar	1½ tbsp.	25 mL
All-purpose flour	1 tbsp.	15 mL
Dry mustard	½ tsp.	2 mL
Salt	⅛ tsp.	0.5 mL
Milk	½ cup	125 mL
White vinegar	1½ tbsp.	25 mL

Cook potato in water in large saucepan until tender. Drain. Cool enough to handle. Cut into small cubes or dice.

Add first amount of salt and pepper. Toss together well. Cover to keep warm. See Tip, page 38.

Sauté bacon in frying pan for 3 to 4 minutes. Add onion and fry until onion is golden. Drain. Stir into potato. Cover to keep warm.

Mix sugar, flour, mustard and second amount of salt in small saucepan.

Stir in milk and vinegar until smooth. Heat and stir until boiling and thickened. Pour over potato mixture. Toss gently to coat. Makes 4 cups (1 L).

¾ cup (175 mL): 233 Calories; 4.1 g Total Fat; 585 mg Sodium; 7 g Protein; 44 g Carbohydrate; 3 g Dietary Fiber

Pictured on page 89.

Paré Pointer
When a sword swallower is on a diet, he eats pins and needles.

Layered Potato Salad

Decorate with topping and cut vegetables for a spectacular buffet dish. Definitely company fare! Attractive layers that slice easily.

FIRST LAYER		
Envelope unflavored gelatin	¼ oz.	7 g
Water	¾ cup	175 mL
Cans of ham flakes (6½ oz., 184 g, each), with liquid, mashed with fork	2	2
Chopped red onion	⅓ cup	75 mL
Light salad dressing (or mayonnaise)	¼ cup	60 mL
Sweet pickle relish	¼ cup	60 mL
SECOND LAYER		
Envelope unflavored gelatin	¼ oz.	7 g
Water	½ cup	125 mL
Light sour cream	⅓ cup	75 mL
Light salad dressing (or mayonnaise)	⅓ cup	75 mL
White vinegar	2 tsp.	10 mL
Granulated sugar	1 tsp.	5 mL
Salt	¾ tsp.	4 mL
Pepper	⅛ tsp.	0.5 mL
Peeled, cooked, diced waxy potatoes	3 cups	750 mL
Diced celery	½ cup	125 mL
Thinly sliced radish	⅓ cup	75 mL
Chopped green onion	⅓ cup	75 mL
Large hard-boiled eggs, chopped	3	3
TOPPING (optional)		
Light cream cheese, softened	8 oz.	250 g
Light salad dressing (or mayonnaise)	2 tbsp.	30 mL
Chopped fresh parsley, for garnish		
Grated or cut fresh vegetables, for garnish		

First Layer: Sprinkle gelatin over water in small saucepan. Let stand for 1 minute. Heat and stir to dissolve. Cool to room temperature.

Stir ham, onion, salad dressing and relish in small bowl. Add gelatin mixture. Stir. Turn into greased 9 x 5 x 3 inch (22 x 12.5 x 7.5 cm) plastic wrap-lined loaf pan. Chill until set.

(continued on next page)

Second Layer: Sprinkle gelatin over water in small saucepan. Let stand for 1 minute. Heat and stir to dissolve. Cool to room temperature.

Stir next 6 ingredients in large bowl. Add gelatin mixture. Stir.

Add potato, celery, radish, onion and egg. Stir. Turn into pan over first layer. Chill several hours or overnight to set until firm. Turn out of pan onto serving plate. Remove plastic wrap.

Topping: Beat cream cheese and salad dressing until fluffy. Spread decoratively over top and sides of loaf. Garnish with parsley and/or vegetables. Serves 8.

¾ cup (175 mL): 346 Calories; 16.1 g Total Fat; 1097 mg Sodium; 13 g Protein; 19 g Carbohydrate; 1 g Dietary Fiber

Pictured on front cover.

Dilly Potato Salad

Substitute dill weed with 1½ to 2 teaspoons (7 to 10 mL) fresh chopped dill if available for a wonderfully fresh taste.

Peeled, cooked, cubed waxy potatoes	4 cups	1 L
Light salad dressing (or mayonnaise)	½ cup	125 mL
Milk	2 tbsp.	30 mL
Green onions, chopped	3	3
Dill weed	½ tsp.	2 mL
Salt	½ tsp.	2 mL
Pepper	⅛ tsp.	0.5 mL

Place potato in large bowl.

Mix remaining 6 ingredients in small bowl. Add to potato. Toss gently to coat well. Chill for 1½ to 2 hours to blend flavors. Makes 4½ cups (1.1 L).

¾ cup (175 mL): 180 Calories; 5.5 g Total Fat; 397 mg Sodium; 3 g Protein; 31 g Carbohydrate; 2 g Dietary Fiber

Potato Salad

A basic, creamy potato salad containing hard-boiled eggs.

Peeled, cooked, diced waxy potatoes	4 cups	1 L
Large hard-boiled eggs, chopped	2	2
Chopped red onion (optional)	¼ cup	60 mL
Green onions, chopped	2	2
Light salad dressing (or mayonnaise)	⅓ cup	75 mL
Lemon juice	1 tbsp.	15 mL
Granulated sugar	1 tbsp.	15 mL
Prepared mustard	1 tsp.	5 mL
Salt	¾ tsp.	4 mL
Pepper	⅛ tsp.	0.5 mL
Milk	2 tbsp.	30 mL

Combine first 4 ingredients in large bowl.

Mix remaining 7 ingredients in small bowl. Pour over potato mixture. Toss gently to coat well. Chill for 1 to 2 hours before serving. Makes 6 cups (1.5 L).

¾ cup (175 mL): 128 Calories; 4.2 g Total Fat; 356 mg Sodium; 3 g Protein; 20 g Carbohydrate; 1 g Dietary Fiber

---

Paré Pointer

If you are invited to a friend's house for a rabbit dinner, it might be lettuce, peas and carrots.

Gnocchi With Sauce

Parmesan sauce and chewy NYOH-kee make a satisfying meal with a crisp, green salad.

Water	½ cup	125 mL
Milk	½ cup	125 mL
Salt	¼ tsp.	1 mL
Cayenne pepper	¹⁄₁₆ tsp.	0.5 mL
Instant potato flakes	1¼ cups	300 mL
Large egg	1	1
All-purpose flour, approximately	½ cup	125 mL
Boiling water	4 qts.	4 L
Salt	1 tbsp.	15 mL
PARMESAN SAUCE		
Margarine (or butter)	2 tbsp.	30 mL
All-purpose flour	2 tbsp.	30 mL
Milk	1 cup	250 mL
Pizza (or spaghetti) sauce	2 tbsp.	30 mL
Salt	¼ tsp.	1 mL
Garlic powder, just a pinch		
Grated Parmesan cheese	⅓ cup	75 mL

Combine first 4 ingredients in medium saucepan. Bring to a boil. Add potato flakes. Mix.

Stir in egg until mixed well. Work in enough flour to form soft dough. Turn out onto lightly floured surface. Roll into ropes ½ inch (12 mm) thick. Cut into ¾ inch (2 cm) pieces. Pinch ends of each piece if desired to emphasize the shape. Keep covered with tea towel as they are made.

Drop all at once into boiling water and salt. Boil for about 3 minutes. Will rise to top when done. Drain. Keep warm in medium bowl. Makes 2½ cups (625 mL) gnocchi.

Parmesan Sauce: Melt margarine in small saucepan. Stir in flour until smooth. Slowly stir in milk. Heat and stir until boiling and thickened. Add remaining 4 ingredients. Stir. Pour over gnocchi. Makes 1⅓ cups (325 mL) sauce. Serves 2 as main dish and 4 as appetizer.

1 main dish serving: 564 Calories; 22.2 g Total Fat; 4876 mg Sodium; 24 g Protein; 67 g Carbohydrate; 8 g Dietary Fiber

Meaty Roulade

Like a giant sausage roll! Elegant to serve for company.
Add a salad and your meal is complete.

MEAT FILLING		
Finely chopped onion	1 cup	250 mL
Chopped fresh mushrooms	2 cups	500 mL
Margarine (or butter)	1 tbsp.	15 mL
Lean ground beef	1 lb.	454 g
Finely chopped red pepper	⅓ cup	75 mL
All-purpose flour	¼ cup	60 mL
Salt	1 tsp.	5 mL
Pepper	¼ tsp.	1 mL
Dried thyme	½ tsp.	2 mL
Light sour cream	½ cup	125 mL
POTATO FILLING		
Light cream cheese, softened	4 oz.	125 g
Large egg	1	1
Mashed potatoes	1 cup	250 mL
Salt	½ tsp.	2 mL
Frozen puff pastry, thawed according to package directions	14.1 oz.	397 g

Meat Filling: Sauté onion and mushrooms in margarine in frying pan until onion is golden. Transfer to small bowl.

Add ground beef and red pepper to frying pan. Scramble-fry until no pink remains in beef. Drain.

Sprinkle with flour, salt, pepper and thyme. Mix well. Add sour cream. Stir until thickened. Add mushroom mixture. Stir. Set aside.

Potato Filling: Beat cream cheese and egg together in large bowl until smooth. Add potatoes and salt. Mix well.

Roll 1 square of puff pastry to 15 inch (38 cm) square. Spread ½ of potato mixture along bottom ⅓ of pastry, about 1 inch (2.5 cm) from edges. Spread ½ of meat mixture on top of potato mixture. Roll up from side with potato like jelly roll. Roll slightly to seal edges. Pinch to seal sides. Place seam side down on ungreased baking sheet. Cut slits decoratively in top to allow steam to escape. Repeat with remaining filling and pastry. Bake in 400°F (205°C) oven for 35 to 40 minutes until golden brown and crisp. Serves 8.

(continued on next page)

1 serving: 379 Calories; 20.4 g Total Fat; 1121 mg Sodium; 18 g Protein; 32 g Carbohydrate; 1 g Dietary Fiber

Pictured on page 35.

To Make Ahead: Bake and cool. Wrap well in plastic wrap, then foil. Label and freeze. To serve, thaw. Reheat in 350°F (175°C) oven until crisp and hot.

Tater-Topped Beef Bake

A variation on an old favorite makes a quick shepherd's pie-type meal to serve a crowd.

Lean ground beef	2 lbs.	900 g
Chopped onion	1 cup	250 mL
Can of condensed cream of mushroom soup	10 oz.	284 mL
Can of condensed cream of chicken soup	10 oz.	284 mL
Milk	1 cup	250 mL
Salt	1 tsp.	5 mL
Pepper	¼ tsp.	1 mL
Package of frozen potato tots, gems or puffs	2.2 lbs.	1 kg
Grated light sharp Cheddar cheese	1 cup	250 mL

Scramble-fry ground beef and onion in non-stick frying pan until no pink remains in beef. Drain.

Combine both soups, milk, salt and pepper in large bowl. Stir vigorously. Stir in beef mixture. Turn into greased 9 x 13 inch (22 x 33 cm) pan.

Arrange frozen potatoes over meat mixture to cover in single layer. Bake, uncovered, in 350°F (175°C) oven for 1 hour.

Sprinkle with cheese. Bake for 15 minutes. Serves 8.

1 serving: 586 Calories; 31.1 g Total Fat; 2028 mg Sodium; 31 g Protein; 47 g Carbohydrate; 4 g Dietary Fiber

Potatoes Bolognese

Quick and easy meat-and-potatoes fare.

Chopped onion	1 cup	250 mL
Lean ground beef	1 lb.	454 g
Bacon slices, diced	2	2
Grated carrot	½ cup	125 mL
Diced celery	¼ cup	60 mL
Chili sauce	¼ cup	60 mL
Milk	⅔ cup	150 mL
Red (or alcohol-free) wine	¼ cup	60 mL
Chopped fresh mushrooms	½ cup	125 mL
Salt	¼ tsp.	1 mL
Worcestershire sauce (optional)	1 tsp.	5 mL
Potatoes (about 3 medium), peeled and cubed	1½ lbs.	680 g
Water		
Grated Parmesan cheese	2 tsp.	10 mL

Sauté onion, ground beef and bacon in large saucepan until no pink remains in beef. Drain.

Add next 8 ingredients. Stir. Cover. Simmer for 30 minutes. Makes 2 cups (500 mL).

Cook potato in water in medium saucepan until tender. Drain. Shake gently over heat to dry. Turn into shallow bowl. Pour sauce on top.

Sprinkle with Parmesan cheese. Serves 4.

1 serving: 385 Calories; 12.1 g Total Fat; 569 mg Sodium; 27 g Protein; 40 g Carbohydrate; 4 g Dietary Fiber

Some potatoes darken when cooked due to a chemical reaction between iron and chlorogenic acid, which naturally occurs in potatoes. To prevent darkening when boiling, either cook with their jackets on and peel after if preferred, or add a bit of lemon juice, vinegar or cream of tartar to the water.

Chicken Pot Pie

This can be prepared to the pastry stage up to one day ahead. Rich, full-bodied flavor. Excellent choice.

Boneless, skinless chicken breasts	1 lb.	454 g
Chopped onion	1 cup	250 mL
Water, just to cover		
Sliced carrots, cut ¼ inch (6 mm) thick	2 cups	500 mL
Peeled, cubed potatoes	3 cups	750 mL
Can of condensed cream of potato soup	10 oz.	284 mL
Can of condensed cream of chicken soup	10 oz.	284 mL
Reserved liquid	1 cup	250 mL
Parsley flakes	½ tsp.	2 mL
Poultry seasoning	¼ tsp.	1 mL
Celery salt	⅛ tsp.	0.5 mL
Pepper	¼ tsp.	1 mL
Frozen puff pastry (14.1 oz., 397 g, package), thawed according to package directions	½	½

Cook chicken and onion in water in large saucepan until chicken is tender. Remove chicken with slotted spoon to plate.

Cook carrots in remaining liquid in same saucepan for 4 minutes. Add potato. Cook until carrot and potato are tender. Drain and reserve liquid. Cube or chop chicken. Add to potato mixture.

Stir next 7 ingredients in large bowl until mixed. Add chicken mixture. Stir. Turn into ungreased 3 quart (3 L) casserole.

Roll pastry a bit larger than casserole diameter. Lay over top. Press pastry up sides all around. Make several slits in top. Bake in 400°F (205°C) oven for 40 minutes until hot and golden brown. Serves 6.

1 serving: 365 Calories; 12.7 g Total Fat; 1170 mg Sodium; 22 g Protein; 41 g Carbohydrate; 3 g Dietary Fiber

To Make Ahead: Top with pastry. Chill. To serve, bake in 400°F (205°C) oven 50 to 60 minutes until hot and golden brown.

Dumpling Casserole

Tender biscuits on a creamy chicken and ham base. Great casual company dish.

Chopped onion	1 cup	250 mL
Chopped celery	1 cup	250 mL
Cooking oil	1 tbsp.	15 mL
Sliced fresh mushrooms	1 cup	250 mL
All-purpose flour	¼ cup	60 mL
Chicken bouillon powder	2 tsp.	10 mL
Pepper	¼ tsp.	1 mL
Water	1 cup	250 mL
Milk	1½ cups	375 mL
Seasoned salt	½ tsp.	2 mL
Cooked, cubed chicken	3 cups	750 mL
Cooked, cubed ham	1 cup	250 mL
SWEET POTATO DUMPLINGS		
All-purpose flour	1½ cups	375 mL
Baking powder	1 tbsp.	15 mL
Ground nutmeg	¼ tsp.	1 mL
Ground cinnamon	¼ tsp.	1 mL
Salt	½ tsp.	2 mL
Large egg, fork-beaten	1	1
Mashed sweet potatoes	2 cups	500 mL
Cooking oil	⅓ cup	75 mL
Milk	¾ cup	175 mL

Sauté onion and celery in cooking oil in frying pan for about 5 minutes until soft.

Add mushrooms. Sauté until soft.

Mix flour, bouillon powder and pepper in small bowl. Gradually whisk in water until smooth. Add milk and seasoned salt. Stir into onion mixture until boiling and thickened.

Combine chicken and ham in ungreased 3 quart (3 L) casserole. Add sauce mixture. Stir to combine.

(continued on next page)

Sweet Potato Dumplings: Combine first 5 ingredients in medium bowl.

Beat egg, sweet potato, cooking oil and milk in small bowl until smooth. Stir into dry ingredients just until moistened. Drop by tablespoonfuls (15 mL) over top of chicken mixture. Bake, uncovered, in 400°F (205°C) oven for 45 minutes until browned. Serves 8.

1 serving: 471 Calories; 18 g Total Fat; 776 mg Sodium; 26 g Protein; 50 g Carbohydrate; 4 g Dietary Fiber

Pictured on page 36.

Shepherd's Pie

A good basic recipe with a colorful mix of vegetables.

Potatoes (about 5 medium), peeled and cut up	2½ lbs.	1.1 kg
Water		
Light sour cream	1 cup	250 mL
Salt	1 tsp.	5 mL
Pepper	¼ tsp.	1 mL
Lean ground beef	2 lbs.	900 g
Chopped onion	1½ cups	375 mL
Beef bouillon powder	1 tsp.	5 mL
Pepper	¼ tsp.	1 mL
Can of condensed cream of mushroom soup	10 oz.	284 mL
Milk	½ cup	125 mL
Frozen mixed vegetables, thawed	4 cups	1 L

Cook potato in water in large saucepan until tender. Drain. Mash.

Mix next 3 ingredients. Mash well.

Sauté ground beef, onion, bouillon powder and pepper in non-stick frying pan until beef is browned. Drain.

Stir soup and milk vigorously in large bowl. Add meat mixture. Stir. Add vegetables. Stir. Turn into ungreased 9 × 13 inch (22 × 33 cm) pan. Pipe, mound or spread potatoes over top. Bake, uncovered, in 375°F (190°C) oven for about 40 minutes until lightly browned and heated through. Serves 10.

1 serving: 343 Calories; 11.9 g Total Fat; 656 mg Sodium; 22 g Protein; 38 g Carbohydrate; 5 g Dietary Fiber

Moussaka

Different and delicious. Good with either beef or lamb. Garnish with eggplant slice, grape tomatoes, rosemary sprig and mint leaves.

Unpeeled medium eggplant, cut into ½ inch (12 mm) slices	1	1
Water		
Salt	½ tsp.	2 mL
Potatoes, (about 4 medium), peeled and cut into ½ inch (12 mm) slices	2 lbs.	900 g
Water		
Salt	½ tsp.	2 mL
Lean ground lamb (or beef)	1½ lbs.	680 g
Chopped onion	1 cup	250 mL
Salt	1 tsp.	5 mL
Pepper	½ tsp.	2 mL
Ground thyme	⅛ tsp.	0.5 mL
Ground nutmeg	⅛ tsp.	0.5 mL
Ground cinnamon	⅛ tsp.	0.5 mL
Garlic powder	¼ tsp.	1 mL
Can of tomatoes, with juice, broken up	14 oz.	398 mL
Grated part-skim mozzarella cheese	1 cup	250 mL
Grated light sharp Cheddar cheese	½ cup	125 mL

Cook eggplant in first amount of water and salt in medium saucepan until tender. Drain well.

Cook potato in second amount of water and salt in large saucepan until just tender. Don't overcook. Drain well.

Scramble-fry ground lamb and onion in non-stick frying pan until browned. Drain.

Add next 7 ingredients to lamb mixture. Stir. Layer eggplant in bottom of greased 9 × 13 inch (22 × 33 cm) pan. Spread ½ of lamb mixture on top. Cover with potato slices, overlapping. Top with remaining ½ of meat mixture.

Sprinkle with mozzarella, then Cheddar cheese. Bake in 350°F (175°C) oven for about 30 minutes until heated through and cheese is melted. Serves 8.

1 serving: 217 Calories; 7.5 g Total Fat; 572 mg Sodium; 18 g Protein; 20 g Carbohydrate; 2 g Dietary Fiber

Pictured on page 54.

Tourtière Turnovers

A nontraditional way to have tourtière. Easy to eat out of your hand. Makes a great appetizer.

Lean ground pork	½ lb.	225 g
Finely chopped onion	⅓ cup	75 mL
Peeled, diced potato	2 cups	500 mL
Parsley flakes	1 tsp.	5 mL
Dried savory leaves	½ tsp.	2 mL
Celery salt	¼ tsp.	1 mL
Salt	1 tsp.	5 mL
Pepper	¼ tsp.	1 mL
Ground nutmeg	¹⁄₁₆ tsp.	0.5 mL
Bay leaf	1	1
Water	1 cup	250 mL
Pastry for a 2 crust pie, your own or a mix		
Large egg, fork-beaten	1	1
Milk	1 tbsp.	15 mL

Combine first 11 ingredients in large saucepan. Heat on medium-high, stirring frequently, until boiling. Reduce heat to medium-low. Cover. Heat for 45 minutes until liquid has absorbed and potatoes are very soft. Discard bay leaf. Stir together very well until smooth. Cool. Makes 2½ cups (625 mL) filling.

Roll ¼ of pastry thinly into 8 × 8 inch (20 × 20 cm) rectangle on floured surface. Cut into four 4 × 4 inch (10 × 10 cm) squares. Place about 2½ tbsp. (37 mL) filling to one side of center on diagonal of each square.

Beat egg and milk together in small dish. Brush 2 adjoining edges of filling side of pastry with egg wash to moisten. Fold unmoistened side diagonally over filling. Crimp to seal. Repeat with remaining pastry and filling. Cut slits in top of pastry. Brush with egg wash. Bake on ungreased baking sheet in 375°F (190°C) oven for 40 minutes until golden brown. Makes 16 turnovers.

1 turnover: 120 Calories; 6.3 g Total Fat; 303 mg Sodium; 5 g Protein; 11 g Carbohydrate; 1 g Dietary Fiber

Pictured on page 53.

Cheesy Potatoes And Wieners

*Good and inexpensive basic food that kids will love.
Serve with a salad for a complete meal.*

Potatoes (about 4 medium), peeled and cut into thin slices	2 lbs.	900 g
Wieners, sliced ½ inch (12 mm) thick	1 lb.	454 g
Grated light sharp Cheddar cheese	1 cup	250 mL
All-purpose flour	2 tbsp.	30 mL
Onion powder	½ tsp.	2 mL
Salt	1 tsp.	5 mL
Pepper	⅛ tsp.	0.5 mL
Milk	1¾ cups	425 mL

Lay ½ of potato in greased shallow 2 quart (2 L) casserole. Layer wieners, cheese and remaining potato.

Measure flour, onion powder, salt and pepper into medium saucepan. Gradually whisk in milk until smooth. Heat and stir until boiling and thickened. Pour over casserole. Poke down a few times with knife to allow sauce to penetrate without disturbing layers. Cover. Bake in 350°F (175°C) oven for 45 minutes. Remove cover. Bake for 15 minutes until potatoes are tender. Serves 4.

1 serving: 635 Calories; 44.3 g Total Fat; 2198 mg Sodium; 27 g Protein; 32 g Carbohydrate; 2 g Dietary Fiber

1. Potato Cake, page 94
2. Tourtière Turnovers, page 51

Props Courtesy Of: Le Gnome

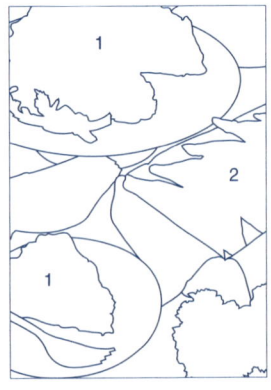

Bean Potato Bake

Substitute sharp Cheddar cheese in place of Havarti for a slight change in flavor.

Light sour cream	½ cup	125 mL
Light salad dressing (or mayonnaise)	¼ cup	60 mL
Milk	¼ cup	60 mL
Prepared mustard	½ tsp.	2 mL
Lemon juice	½ tsp.	2 mL
Prepared horseradish	½ tsp.	2 mL
Sherry (or alcohol-free sherry)	1 tbsp.	15 mL
Minced onion flakes	1 tbsp.	15 mL
Salt	1 tsp.	5 mL
Pepper	⅛ tsp.	0.5 mL
Can of pinto beans, drained	14 oz.	398 mL
Peeled, cooked, cubed potatoes	2 cups	500 mL
Grated Havarti cheese	1 cup	250 mL

Mix first 10 ingredients in large bowl.

Add beans, potato and cheese. Stir. Turn into ungreased 1½ quart (1.5 L) casserole. Bake, uncovered, in 350°F (175°C) oven for about 40 minutes until hot. Serves 4.

1 serving: 332 Calories; 14.5 g Total Fat; 1188 mg Sodium; 14.5 g Protein; 36 g Carbohydrate; 3 g Dietary Fiber

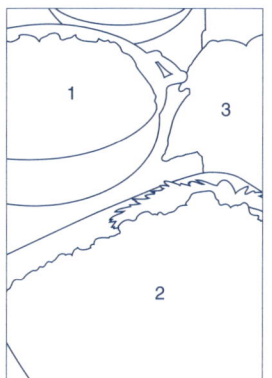

1. Tomato Potato Casserole, page 66
2. Moussaka, page 50
3. Potato Buns, page 27

Props Courtesy Of: Le Gnome
The Bay

Main Dishes

Pizza Hash Brown

Hash browns make a great crust. Meat and potatoes in a pizza.

HASH BROWN PIZZA CRUST		
Frozen hash brown potatoes, thawed	6 cups	1.5 L
Light sour cream	¾ cup	175 mL
Large eggs	2	2
Powdered Cheddar cheese product	2 tbsp.	30 mL
Salt	1 tsp.	5 mL
Pepper	¼ tsp.	1 mL
Margarine (or butter)	1 tbsp.	15 mL
Chopped onion	1 cup	250 mL
Chili sauce	½ cup	125 mL
Chili powder	½ tsp.	2 mL
Diced pepperoni (or ham or scramble-fried lean ground beef)	1½ cups	375 mL
Grated part-skim mozzarella (or medium Cheddar) cheese, see Note	1½ cups	375 mL

Hash Brown Pizza Crust: Combine all 6 ingredients in large bowl. Mix well. Press firmly in greased 12 inch (30 cm) pizza pan, forming rim around edge. Bake in 450°F (230°C) oven for 20 to 25 minutes. Remove to rack.

Melt margarine in medium frying pan. Add onion. Sauté on medium-low, stirring frequently, until very soft and starting to brown.

Stir in chili sauce, chili powder and pepperoni. Spread over crust.

Sprinkle with cheese. Bake for 5 to 6 minutes until hot and cheese is melted. Cuts into 8 wedges.

1 wedge: 421 Calories; 22.1 g Total Fat; 1354 mg Sodium; 18 g Protein; 39 g Carbohydrate; 5 g Dietary Fiber

Note: A mixture of both cheeses is attractive and tasty.

Paré Pointer

His dog is so loyal that he always comes home after each time he's sold.

Spudonion Pizza

Pretty-as-a-picture pizza. Lots of tangy flavor too!

CRUST		
All-purpose flour	2 cups	500 mL
Instant yeast	1¼ tsp.	6 mL
Salt	¼ tsp.	1 mL
Very warm water	⅔ cup	150 mL
Cooking oil (optional)	2 tbsp.	30 mL
TOPPING		
Medium red onion, coarsely chopped	1	1
Small red pepper, cut into thin strips	1	1
Cooking oil	1 tbsp.	15 mL
Frozen hash brown potatoes	1 cup	250 mL
Non-fat sour cream	½ cup	125 mL
Grated part-skim mozzarella cheese	1½ cups	375 mL

Crust: Put first 3 ingredients into food processor fitted with dough blade. (See below for hand method.) With machine running, pour warm water and cooking oil through tube in lid. Process for 50 to 60 seconds. If dough seems sticky, add about ½ tsp. (2 mL) flour to make it easier to handle.

For regular crust: Roll out dough. Press in greased 12 inch (30 cm) pizza pan, forming rim around edge.

For thick crust: Cover shaped crust with tea towel. Let stand in oven with light on and door closed for about 1 hour until doubled in size.

Topping: Sauté onion and red pepper in cooking oil in frying pan until starting to soften. Stir in hash browns. Sauté for 2 to 3 minutes. Remove from heat.

Spread sour cream over crust.

Sprinkle with ½ cup (125 mL) cheese. Spoon onion mixture over top. Sprinkle with remaining cheese. Bake on bottom rack in 425°F (220°C) oven for 15 minutes. If using partially baked crust, cut baking time to 8 to 10 minutes. Cuts into 8 wedges.

Hand Method: Put first 3 ingredients into medium bowl. Stir together well. Add warm water and cooking oil. Mix well until dough leaves sides of bowl. Knead on lightly floured surface for 5 to 8 minutes until smooth and elastic.

1 wedge: 230 Calories; 5.9 g Total Fat; 206 mg Sodium; 10 g Protein; 33 g Carbohydrate; 2 g Dietary Fiber

Pictured on page 71.

THIN CRUST: Reduce flour to 1½ cups (375 mL) and reduce water to ½ cup (125 mL). Crust will cook a bit quicker.

Seafood Delight

Delicious and attractive. Use your prettiest casserole dish to show off at the table!

Mashed potatoes	3 cups	750 mL
Large eggs, fork-beaten	2	2
Grated light sharp Cheddar cheese	½ cup	125 mL
Pepper, sprinkle		
Paprika, sprinkle		
Margarine (or butter)	2 tbsp.	30 mL
Sliced fresh mushrooms	1 cup	250 mL
All-purpose flour	¼ cup	60 mL
Milk	2 cups	500 mL
White (or alcohol-free) wine	2 tbsp.	30 mL
Grated light sharp Cheddar cheese	1 cup	250 mL
Parsley flakes	½ tsp.	2 mL
Seasoned salt	½ tsp.	2 mL
Pepper, sprinkle		
Cooked shrimp	1½ cups	375 mL
Imitation crab, cut into bite-size chunks	1½ cups	375 mL
(or use 2 cans, 5 oz., 142 g, each, drained)		
Frozen tiny peas, thawed	1 cup	250 mL
Grated light sharp Cheddar cheese	1 cup	250 mL

Combine first 4 ingredients in medium bowl. Mix until smooth. Empty into shallow greased 2 quart (2 L) casserole. Pack bottom and sides with potato mixture. Sprinkle with paprika.

Melt margarine in large saucepan. Add mushrooms. Sauté until golden. Sprinkle with flour. Stir well. Slowly add milk and wine, whisking constantly, until boiling and thickened.

Stir in second amount of cheese, parsley, seasoned salt and pepper. Remove from heat.

Stir in shrimp, crab and peas. Pour into potato-lined casserole.

Cover with third amount of cheese. Bake in 350°F (175°C) oven for 30 minutes until hot and bubbling. Serves 6.

1 serving: 502 Calories; 17.9 g Total Fat; 732 mg Sodium; 45 g Protein; 36 g Carbohydrate; 3 g Dietary Fiber

Shrimp Pot Pie

Excellent presentation with great flavor.

Unpeeled potatoes (about 3 medium)	1½ lbs.	680 g
Water		
All-purpose flour	6 tbsp.	100 mL
Salt	1 tsp.	5 mL
Pepper	⅛ tsp.	0.5 mL
Milk	2 cups	500 mL
Light mayonnaise (or salad dressing)	½ cup	125 mL
Frozen peas	1 cup	250 mL
Small fresh (or cooked) shrimp, rinsed and drained	6 oz.	170 g
Frozen puff pastry (14.1 oz., 397 g, package), thawed according to package directions	½	½

Cook whole potatoes in water in medium saucepan until just tender. Drain. Cool enough to handle. Peel and cube.

Stir flour, salt and pepper in large saucepan. Gradually whisk in milk until smooth. Stir in mayonnaise. Heat and stir until boiling and thickened. Add potatoes, peas and shrimp. Stir. Turn into ungreased 2 quart (2 L) casserole.

Roll pastry a bit larger than casserole diameter. Lay over top. Press pastry up sides all around. Make several slits in top. Bake in 400°F (205°C) oven for 30 to 35 minutes until hot and golden brown. Serves 4.

1 serving: 525 Calories; 21.5 g Total Fat; 1501 mg Sodium; 21 g Protein; 62 g Carbohydrate; 4 g Dietary Fiber

To Make Ahead: Prepare to pastry stage. Chill. To serve, top with pastry. Bake for 50 to 60 minutes until hot and golden brown.

For crispier french fries, use baking (old) potatoes. Waxy (new) potatoes will not brown or crisp as well. If you choose to use waxy potatoes, cut them and soak in cold water, then drain and pat dry before deep-frying.

Fish Cakes

Traditional fare from Atlantic coastal villages uses salt cod. Serve with tartar sauce.

Cod fillet	½ lb.	225 g
Water, to cover		
Large egg	1	1
Mashed potatoes	2 cups	500 mL
Soda cracker crumbs	2 tbsp.	30 mL
Lemon juice	1 tsp.	5 mL
Onion powder	¼ tsp.	1 mL
Parsley flakes	1 tsp.	5 mL
Salt	¼ tsp.	1 mL
Pepper	¹⁄₁₆ tsp.	0.5 mL
Fine dry bread crumbs	⅓ cup	75 mL
Margarine (or butter)	2 tbsp.	30 mL

Simmer fish in water in medium saucepan for about 8 minutes until flaky. Drain. Flake fish in medium bowl.

Add next 8 ingredients. Mix well. Shape into patties using about ¼ cup (60 mL) each.

Coat patties with bread crumbs.

Melt 1 tbsp. (15 mL) margarine in large non-stick frying pan. Brown patties on one side, about 4 to 5 minutes. Remove to plate. Melt remaining margarine in pan. Turn cakes and fry second side until crispy brown. Makes 8 cakes.

1 cake: 132 Calories; 4.2 g Total Fat; 194 mg Sodium; 8 g Protein; 16 g Carbohydrate; 1 g Dietary Fiber

Paré Pointer
There is a big difference between a grand baby and a baby grand.

Potato Stuffing

Nice mix of potato and stuffing flavors in this great baked side dish!
Or stuff your bird with it at holiday time.

Cooking oil	2 tsp.	10 mL
Chopped onion	1 cup	250 mL
Chopped celery	½ cup	125 mL
Ground savory	1 tsp.	5 mL
Poultry seasoning	½ tsp.	2 mL
Salt	1½ tsp.	7 mL
Pepper	¼ tsp.	1 mL
Mashed potatoes	3½ cups	875 mL
Dry bread crumbs	2½ cups	625 mL
Chicken bouillon powder	1 tsp.	5 mL
Hot water	½ cup	125 mL

Heat cooking oil in frying pan. Add onion and celery. Sauté until soft.

Season with next 4 ingredients.

Combine potato and bread crumbs in large bowl. Add onion mixture. Stir.

Dissolve bouillon in water. Slowly add to potato mixture. Mix well until stuffing holds together when squeezed lightly. Add more water, a little bit at a time, if necessary. Turn into greased 2 quart (2 L) casserole. Cover. Bake in 350°F (175°C) oven for 45 to 60 minutes until heated through. Makes 8½ cups (2.1 L).

½ cup (125 mL): 117 Calories; 1.4 g Total Fat; 408 mg Sodium; 3 g Protein; 23 g Carbohydrate; 1 g Dietary Fiber

Paré Pointer

When the cow mooed twice at the little boy, he shouted:
"She blew both her horns."

Creamed Veggies

One-bowl potatoes and vegetables are very quick to prepare.

Unpeeled baby potatoes (or about 3 unpeeled medium new potatoes, cut up)	1½ lbs.	680 g
Water		
Fresh or frozen baby carrots	2 cups	500 mL
Frozen peas	2 cups	500 mL
CREAM SAUCE		
Milk	1½ cups	375 mL
All-purpose four	3 tbsp.	50 mL
Salt	½ tsp.	2 mL
Pepper	⅛ tsp.	0.5 mL
Onion powder	⅛ tsp.	0.5 mL

Cook potatoes in water in large saucepan for about 10 minutes until almost tender.

Add carrots. Cook for 3 minutes until tender.

Add peas. Cook for 2 minutes. Drain. Keep warm.

Cream Sauce: Whisk milk into flour, salt, pepper and onion powder in medium saucepan until smooth. Heat and stir until boiling and thickened. Pour vegetables into serving bowl. Gently combine with cream sauce. Serves 6.

1 serving: 202 Calories; 1.1 g Total Fat; 343 mg Sodium; 8 g Protein; 41 g Carbohydrate; 6 g Dietary Fiber

Glazed Garlic Potatoes

These golden potatoes are excellent with a roast pork or beef.

White (or alcohol-free) wine	⅓ cup	75 mL
Virgin olive oil	3 tbsp.	50 mL
Finely chopped onion	⅓ cup	75 mL
Garlic cloves, finely chopped (not minced)	4	4
Dried rosemary, crushed	½ tsp.	2 mL
Dried thyme	¼ tsp.	1 mL
Salt	½ tsp.	2 mL
Freshly ground pepper	⅛ tsp.	0.5 mL
Unpeeled baby potatoes (or about 6 unpeeled medium new potatoes, cut up)	3 lbs.	1.4 kg

(continued on next page)

Combine first 8 ingredients in small saucepan. Bring to a boil. Pour into medium roasting pan.

Add potatoes. Stir to coat with spice mixture. Roast, uncovered, in 400°F (205°C) oven for about 60 minutes until tender. Stir and shake potatoes several times while roasting. Serves 8.

1 serving: 183 Calories; 5.3 g Total Fat; 183 mg Sodium; 4 g Protein; 29 g Carbohydrate; 3 g Dietary Fiber

Savory New Potatoes

Lots of creamy mustard sauce gives baby potatoes a wonderful taste. Try substituting a nice grainy mustard for the prepared mustard.

Unpeeled baby potatoes (or about 4 unpeeled medium new potatoes, cubed)	2 lbs.	900 g
Water		
Salt	½ tsp.	2 mL
All-purpose flour	2 tbsp.	30 mL
Granulated sugar	1 tbsp.	15 mL
Salt	½ tsp.	2 mL
Pepper	⅛ tsp.	0.5 mL
Large egg	1	1
Prepared mustard	1-2 tsp.	5-10 mL
Milk	1 cup	250 mL
White vinegar	1 tbsp.	15 mL

Cook potatoes in water and first amount of salt in large saucepan until tender. Drain.

Mix flour, sugar, second amount of salt and pepper in small saucepan.

Mix in egg until smooth. Add mustard and milk. Heat and stir until boiling and thickened.

Stir in vinegar. Pour over potatoes in serving bowl. Toss gently to coat. Serves 6.

1 serving: 179 Calories; 1.5 g Total Fat; 278 mg Sodium; 6 g Protein; 37 g Carbohydrate; 3 g Dietary Fiber

New Potato Treat

Creamy, coated baby potatoes with dill make these extra special.

Unpeeled baby potatoes (or about 4 unpeeled medium potatoes, cubed)	2 lbs.	900 g
Salt	¼ tsp.	1 mL
Water		
Light sour cream	½ cup	125 mL
Green onions, chopped	3-4	3-4
Dill weed	½ tsp.	2 mL
Salt	¼ tsp.	1 mL
Pepper	¼ tsp.	1 mL

Cook potatoes in salted water in large saucepan until tender. Drain.

Add remaining 5 ingredients. Place on still-hot burner and shake saucepan or gently stir contents until heated through. Serves 6.

1 serving: 149 Calories; 1.6 g Total Fat; 130 mg Sodium; 4 g Protein; 31 g Carbohydrate; 3 g Dietary Fiber

Tiny Herb Garlic Spuds

Fresh-tasting with crispy skins. Easy and quick.

Unpeeled tiny baby potatoes	16	16
Water		
Margarine (or butter)	2 tbsp.	30 mL
Garlic clove(s), minced	1-2	1-2
Chopped fresh parsley	2 tbsp.	30 mL
Chopped chives	1 tbsp.	15 mL
Salt	¼ tsp.	1 mL
Pepper, sprinkle		

Cook potatoes in water in medium saucepan until tender. Drain.

Melt margarine in frying pan. Add garlic, parsley, chives, salt and pepper. Heat and stir until garlic is tender. Add potatoes. Stir to coat. Heat, stirring often, for 3 to 5 minutes. Serves 4.

1 serving: 184 Calories; 6 g Total Fat; 247 mg Sodium; 3 g Protein; 31 g Carbohydrate; 3 g Dietary Fiber

Pictured on front cover.

Jalapeño Potatoes

Pimiento and hah-lah-PEH-nyohs add a nice color contrast to the pale orange sauce. If you dare, use the whole can of jalapeño peppers! For that added touch, garnish with green and orange jalapeños.

Milk	2 cups	500 mL
All-purpose flour	3 tbsp.	50 mL
Salt	1 tsp.	5 mL
Pepper	¼ tsp.	1 mL
Garlic powder	¼ tsp.	1 mL
Grated light sharp Cheddar cheese	1 cup	250 mL
Can of chopped jalapeño peppers (4 oz., 114 mL, drained) or ⅛-¼ cup (30-60 mL) chopped, drained hot mixed peppers	½	½
Unpeeled waxy potatoes (about 4 medium)	2 lbs.	900 g
Water		
Jar of chopped pimiento, drained	2 oz.	57 mL

Gradually whisk milk into flour, salt, pepper and garlic powder in medium saucepan until smooth. Heat and stir until boiling and thickened.

Add cheese and jalapeño peppers. Stir to melt cheese. Set aside.

Cook whole potatoes in water in large saucepan for 15 to 18 minutes until just tender. Drain. Cool enough to handle. Peel. Slice thinly. Place in large bowl.

Add cheese sauce and pimiento. Stir. Turn into greased 2 quart (2 L) casserole. Bake, uncovered, in 350°F (175°C) oven for about 30 minutes until potato is tender. Serves 6.

1 serving: 176 Calories; 4.6 g Total Fat; 606 mg Sodium; 9 g Protein; 25 g Carbohydrate; 2 g Dietary Fiber

Pictured on page 72.

When chopping jalapeños use gloves, as the caustic oily compounds called capsaicin (kap-SAY-ih-sihn), permeate the skin and can actually cause a burning sensation. Also, keep your gloved hands away from your eyes.

Side Dishes

Potato Mushroom Bake

If you like mushrooms you'll love the rich flavor of this casserole.

Peeled, cubed potatoes	5 cups	1.25 L
Sliced fresh mushrooms	3 cups	750 mL
All-purpose flour	¼ cup	60 mL
Dried sweet basil	⅛ tsp.	0.5 mL
Garlic powder	⅛ tsp.	0.5 mL
Dried whole oregano	⅛ tsp.	0.5 mL
Salt	¼ tsp.	1 mL
Pepper	⅛ tsp.	0.5 mL
Can of condensed chicken broth	10 oz.	284 mL
Grated Swiss cheese	1 cup	250 mL

Combine potato and mushrooms in greased 3 quart (3 L) casserole.

Combine next 6 ingredients in medium saucepan. Slowly whisk in chicken broth until smooth. Heat and stir, until boiling and thickened. Pour over potato mixture. Stir gently. Bake, uncovered, in 350°F (175°C) oven for 1 hour.

Sprinkle casserole with cheese. Bake for 20 minutes until potato is tender. Serves 8.

1 serving: 113 Calories; 4.3 g Total Fat; 296 mg Sodium; 7 g Protein; 12 g Carbohydrate; 1 g Dietary Fiber

Tomato Potato Casserole

Evident potato, tomato and cheese layers with a bit of an Italian flavor. Serves a crowd. Makes a great potluck or buffet dinner presentation.

Potatoes (about 6 medium), peeled and sliced	3 lbs.	1.4 kg
Medium onions, sliced	4	4
Medium tomatoes, sliced	4	4
Grated Monterey Jack cheese	¾ cup	175 mL
Grated light Parmesan cheese	½ cup	125 mL
Dried whole oregano, crushed	½ tsp.	2 mL
Dried sweet basil	½ tsp.	2 mL
Salt	1 tsp.	5 mL
Pepper	¼ tsp.	1 mL
Grated part-skim mozzarella cheese	1 cup	250 mL

(continued on next page)

Layer ½ of first 3 ingredients in greased 4 quart (4 L) casserole. Sprinkle with all of Monterey Jack cheese.

Mix Parmesan cheese, oregano, basil, salt and pepper in small bowl. Sprinkle ½ over Jack cheese. Layer second ½ of vegetables over top. Sprinkle with second ½ of Parmesan and herb mixture.

Scatter mozzarella cheese over top. Cover. Bake in 400°F (205°C) oven for about 50 minutes. Remove cover. Bake for about 10 minutes until potatoes are tender. Serves 8.

1 serving: 202 Calories; 7.2 g Total Fat; 599 mg Sodium; 12 g Protein; 24 g Carbohydrate; 3 g Dietary Fiber

Pictured on page 54.

Oven Potatoes Lyonnaise

Recipe is easily doubled—use a small roaster and cook a bit longer until potatoes are tender. Try the variation below for a non-fat alternative.

Medium onion, chopped or sliced	1	1
Potatoes (about 3 medium), peeled and cut into ¼ inch (6 mm) thick slices	1½ lbs.	680 g
Margarine (or butter), melted	3 tbsp.	50 mL
Salt	¼ tsp.	1 mL
Pepper, sprinkle		

Place onion and potato slices in 2 quart (2 L) casserole.

Drizzle with margarine. Sprinkle with salt and pepper. Stir to coat well. Cover. Bake in 350°F (175°C) oven for 1 to 1¼ hours until potato is tender. Serves 4.

1 serving: 149 Calories; 8.2 g Total Fat; 270 mg Sodium; 2 g Protein; 18 g Carbohydrate; 2 g Dietary Fiber

Variation: Omit margarine. Slice onion ¼ inch (6 mm) thick and potatoes ½ inch (12 mm) thick. Place in casserole. Sprinkle with salt and pepper. Stir ½ cup (125 mL) boiling water with 1 tsp. (5 mL) beef bouillon powder in cup. Pour into casserole at outer edge. Cover. Bake in 400°F (205°C) oven for 20 minutes. Remove cover. Bake for 30 to 40 minutes until liquid has almost evaporated and potato is tender.

Hasselback Potatoes

From Stockholm, named after the restaurant where it was first featured.

Medium potatoes, peeled	6	6
Margarine (or butter), melted	¼ cup	60 mL
Fine dry bread crumbs	2 tbsp.	30 mL
Grated light Parmesan cheese	1 tbsp.	15 mL
Salt	½ tsp.	2 mL
Pepper	¹⁄₁₆ tsp.	0.5 mL

Place 1 potato on large spoon. Cut crosswise into ¼ inch (6 mm) thick slices just to edge of spoon, leaving bottom of potato uncut. Repeat. Keep cut potatoes covered with cold water in bowl. When all are cut, drain. Pat potatoes dry. Arrange, cut side up, in greased 9 × 13 inch (22 × 33 cm) baking dish.

Brush potatoes with some of margarine. Bake, uncovered, in 425°F (220°C) oven for 30 minutes. Brush with remaining margarine. Bake for 15 minutes.

Combine remaining 4 ingredients in small dish. Sprinkle evenly over potatoes. Bake for 15 minutes until tender and crumbs are golden brown. Serves 6.

1 serving: 168 Calories; 7.9 g Total Fat; 356 mg Sodium; 3 g Protein; 22 g Carbohydrate; 2 g Dietary Fiber

Gratin Dauphinois

Pronounced GRAH-tn doh-FEEN-o, this is quick and easy to put together. Wonderful aroma while cooking.

Garlic clove, halved (optional)	1	1
Potatoes (about 4 medium), peeled and thinly sliced	2 lbs.	900 g
Light cream	1 cup	250 mL
Salt	¼ tsp.	1 mL
Pepper	⅛ tsp.	0.5 mL
Ground nutmeg	¹⁄₁₆ tsp.	0.5 mL
Grated Gruyère cheese	¾ cup	175 mL
Grated Gruyère cheese	⅓ cup	75 mL

(continued on next page)

Rub inside of 2 quart (2 L) casserole with garlic. Spray well with no-stick cooking spray.

Layer potato slices in casserole.

Heat cream, salt, pepper, nutmeg and first amount of cheese in small saucepan until hot. Pour over potato.

Sprinkle with second amount of cheese. Bake, uncovered, in 350°F (175°C) oven for 45 to 50 minutes until potatoes are tender. Serves 6.

1 serving: 195 Calories; 11 g Total Fat; 204 mg Sodium; 9 g Protein; 15 g Carbohydrate; 1 g Dietary Fiber

Scalloped Potatoes

Warm golden in color with a browned crumble topping.

Waxy potatoes (about 6 medium), quartered (see Note)	3 lbs.	1.4 kg
Water		
Light sour cream	¾ cup	175 mL
Can of condensed cream of chicken soup	10 oz.	284 mL
Grated light sharp Cheddar cheese	¼ cup	60 mL
Green onions, sliced	4	4
Prepared mustard	1 tsp.	5 mL
TOPPING		
Margarine (or butter)	2 tbsp.	30 mL
Crushed corn flakes cereal (not corn flakes crumbs)	½ cup	125 mL

Cook potato in water in large saucepan until just tender. Drain. Cool enough to handle. Slice thinly. Put into greased 2 quart (2 L) casserole.

Mix next 5 ingredients in medium saucepan. Heat until cheese is melted. Pour over potato. Mix lightly to distribute some liquid to bottom.

Topping: Melt margarine in small saucepan. Stir in cereal. Sprinkle over top. Bake in 350°F (175°C) oven for about 45 minutes until browned. Serves 6.

1 serving: 227 Calories; 10.2 g Total Fat; 565 mg Sodium; 6 g Protein; 29 g Carbohydrate; 2 g Dietary Fiber

Note: Waxy potatoes are preferred since dry baking potatoes are apt to break up when baked further in oven.

Potatoes Parmesan

Crispy with lots of Parmesan zing.

All-purpose flour	2 tbsp.	30 mL
Grated Parmesan cheese	⅓ cup	75 mL
Paprika	½ tsp.	2 mL
Salt	½ tsp.	2 mL
Pepper	⅛ tsp.	0.5 mL
Potatoes (about 4 medium), peeled and cut into thick slices	2 lbs.	900 g
Margarine (or butter), melted	4 tsp.	20 mL

Combine first 5 ingredients in plastic bag.

Blot potato slices dry. Dip in, or brush with, margarine. Put a few at a time into bag. Shake to coat with flour mixture. Arrange potato slices in single layer on large greased baking sheet. Bake in 350°F (175°C) oven for about 30 minutes until tender. Serves 4.

1 serving: 176 Calories; 6.4 g Total Fat; 551 mg Sodium; 6 g Protein; 24 g Carbohydrate; 2 g Dietary Fiber

Paré Pointer
Baby corn asked the mommy corn where the popcorn was.

1. Spudonion Pizza, page 57
2. Mushroom Cheese Braids, page 96

Props Courtesy Of: Le Gnome

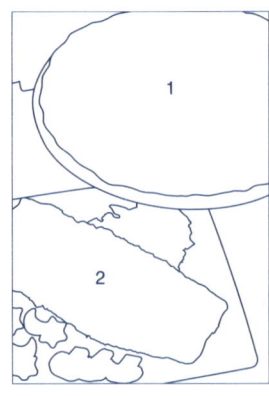

Side Dishes

Quick Scallop Bake

These are very good when served with sour cream.

Unpeeled potatoes (about 5 medium), cut into ¼ inch (6 mm) slices	2½ lbs.	1.1 kg
Minced onion flakes	2 tsp.	10 mL
Margarine (or butter), melted	¼ cup	60 mL
Hot water	1 tbsp.	15 mL
Beef bouillon powder	1 tbsp.	15 mL
Pepper	¹⁄₁₆ tsp.	0.5 mL
Non-fat sour cream (optional)	½ cup	125 mL

Layer potato slices in greased 2 quart (2 L) casserole, sprinkling with minced onion between layers.

Combine margarine, water, beef bouillon and pepper in small cup. Drizzle over casserole. Cover. Bake in 350°F (175°C) oven for 30 minutes. Stir. Cover. Bake for about 30 minutes until potatoes are tender.

Serve with sour cream. Serves 6.

1 serving: 147 Calories; 7.8 g Total Fat; 392 mg Sodium; 3 g Protein; 18 g Carbohydrate; 2 g Dietary Fiber

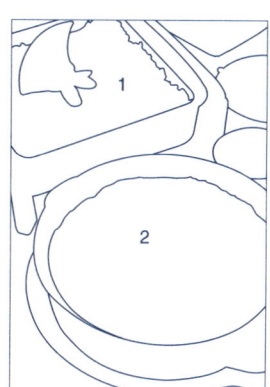

1. Con Queso Potatoes, page 102
2. Jalapeño Potatoes, page 65

Props Courtesy Of: Le Gnome

Side Dishes

Potato Cheese Frittata

This frittata can be done on the stovetop or in the oven. Vary the type of cheese to Swiss, a jalapeño-flavored Jack cheese or a smoked Cheddar for a terrific flavor change.

Potatoes (about 2 medium), peeled and quartered	1 lb.	454 g
Water		
Chopped onion	⅔ cup	150 mL
Cooking oil	1 tsp.	5 mL
Large eggs	3	3
Water	1 tbsp.	15 mL
Parsley flakes	¼ tsp.	1 mL
Paprika	¼ tsp.	1 mL
Salt	¼ tsp.	1 mL
Pepper	⅛ tsp.	0.5 mL
Grated light sharp Cheddar cheese	½ cup	125 mL

Cook potato in water until tender. Drain. Cool enough to handle. Dice.

Sauté onion in cooking oil in non-stick frying pan until tender.

Beat next 6 ingredients in medium bowl until smooth. Stir in potato. Pour over onion in pan. Cover. Cook on medium-low for 9 to 10 minutes until almost set.

Sprinkle with cheese. Put pan under broiler near top of oven (see Tip, below), until cheese is melted and frittata is set on top. Cuts into 4 wedges.

Oven Method: Sauté onion. Combine all ingredients except cheese in greased 1 quart (1 L) casserole dish. Bake, uncovered, at 350°F (175°C) for 20 minutes. Sprinkle with cheese. Bake or broil for 1 to 2 minutes until cheese is melted.

1 wedge: 220 Calories; 8.1 g Total Fat; 319 mg Sodium; 11 g Protein; 26 g Carbohydrate; 2 g Dietary Fiber

POTATO FRITTATA: Omit cheese.

When broiling food in a frying pan and the handle is not ovenproof, keep it to the front of the oven, away from the element.

Sausage Frittata

Generous amounts of sausage and potato.

Sausages	3	3
Cooking oil	1 tsp.	5 mL
Cooking oil	1 tsp.	5 mL
Green onions, chopped	3	3
Cooked, diced potatoes	1 cup	250 mL
Large eggs	6	6
Water	3 tbsp.	50 mL
Seasoned salt	½ tsp.	2 mL
Salt	⅛ tsp.	0.5 mL
Pepper, sprinkle		

Fry sausages in first amount of cooking oil in non-stick frying pan until brown. Drain. Remove sausages. Cut into coins.

Heat second amount of cooking oil in same pan. Add sausage coins, onion and potato. Sauté for 2 minutes. Spread mixture evenly in bottom of pan.

Beat eggs, water, seasoned salt, salt and pepper with fork in medium bowl. Pour over mixture in pan. Cover. Cook on medium-low for about 4 minutes. Using spatula, gently move egg mixture from outer edges towards middle of pan in about 3 places, tipping pan each time to allow unset egg to run into created space. Cover. Cook for 4 minutes until set. Cover frying pan with inverted serving plate. Flip both over so frittata is on plate, browned side up, for serving. Cuts into 6 wedges.

1 wedge: 130 Calories; 8.1 g Total Fat; 287 mg Sodium; 8 g Protein; 6 g Carbohydrate; trace Dietary Fiber

 When you need cooked potato for a recipe in a hurry, use your microwave. Wash and prick potato all over with a fork, wrap in paper towel and microwave on high (100%) 4 to 6 minutes. Turn halfway through cooking. If baking more than one at once, increase cooking time. Cool, peel and chop or mash.

Potato Quiche

Dill and parsley add some pretty flecks to the final look.

Frozen hash brown potatoes	1½ cups	375 mL
Leeks (white part only), chopped	2	2
Margarine (or butter)	1 tbsp.	15 mL
Large eggs	3	3
Skim evaporated milk	1 cup	250 mL
Grated Swiss (or Gruyère) cheese	¾ cup	175 mL
Dill weed	¾ tsp.	4 mL
Parsley flakes	¾ tsp.	4 mL
Seasoned salt	¾ tsp.	4 mL
Pepper	¼ tsp.	1 mL
Ground nutmeg	1/16 tsp.	0.5 mL
Unbaked 9 inch (22 cm) pie shell	1	1

Brown potatoes and leek in margarine in frying pan. Cool.

Beat eggs in medium bowl until smooth. Beat in milk. Add potato mixture, cheese, dill, parsley, seasoned salt, pepper and nutmeg. Stir.

Turn into pastry shell. Bake on bottom rack in 350°F (175°C) oven for 45 minutes until knife inserted in center comes out clean. Cuts into 6 wedges.

1 wedge: 371 Calories; 19.7 g Total Fat; 531 mg Sodium; 14 g Protein; 35 g Carbohydrate; 2 g Dietary Fiber

Spanish Omelet

Red sauce on top makes this attractive for company brunch.

Peeled, cubed potatoes	2 cups	500 mL
Small onion, coarsely chopped	1	1
Olive (or cooking) oil	1 tbsp.	15 mL
Large eggs	6	6
Water	3 tbsp.	50 mL
Seasoned salt	½ tsp.	2 mL
Pepper	¼ tsp.	1 mL
Hot pepper sauce	¼ tsp.	1 mL
Chili sauce (or salsa)	3 tbsp.	50 mL

(continued on next page)

Cook potato and onion in olive oil in non-stick frying pan on medium for about 20 minutes until tender. Turn potato several times to brown.

Beat eggs, water, seasoned salt, pepper and hot pepper sauce in medium bowl. Reduce heat under frying pan to low. Pour egg mixture into pan over potatoes. Cover. Cook on low for 8 minutes until bottom is browned.

Drizzle top with chili sauce. Place under broiler (see Tip, page 74), on top oven rack for 2 minutes until set and golden brown. Cuts into 6 wedges.

1 wedge: 148 Calories; 7.4 g Total Fat; 297 mg Sodium; 8 g Protein; 13 g Carbohydrate; 1 g Dietary Fiber

Pictured on page 18.

Potato Soufflé

Most soufflés won't wait. This one sits in the oven and stays fluffy until ready to serve.

Margarine (or butter), softened	1 tbsp.	15 mL
Grated Parmesan cheese	½ cup	125 mL
Hot mashed potatoes	2 cups	500 mL
Hot milk	½ cup	125 mL
Margarine (or butter)	2 tsp.	10 mL
Chopped fresh parsley (or 1½ tsp., 7 mL, flakes)	2 tbsp.	30 mL
Salt	½ tsp.	2 mL
Pepper	¼ tsp.	1 mL
Egg yolks (large)	3	3
Reserved Parmesan cheese		
Egg whites (large), room temperature	3	3
Cream of tartar	½ tsp.	2 mL

Grease sides and bottom of soufflé dish or 1 quart (1 L) casserole well with margarine. Coat well with Parmesan cheese. Empty excess cheese into small dish and reserve. Preheat oven to 350°F (175°C).

Beat next 8 ingredients in large bowl on low until fluffy.

Beat egg whites with clean beaters in medium bowl until peaks are stiff but not dry. Fold ⅓ of egg whites into potato mixture just until mixed. Fold in remaining egg whites. Turn into prepared soufflé dish. Bake on bottom rack of oven for 35 minutes. Serves 6.

1 serving: 181 Calories; 8.7 g Total Fat; 475 mg Sodium; 9 g Protein; 17 g Carbohydrate; 1 g Dietary Fiber

All-In-One Breakfast

The name says it all! Wonderful bacon and egg frittata with perfect seasoning and good cheese flavor.

Bacon slices, diced	4	4
Chopped onion	½ cup	125 mL
Peeled, cooked, cubed potatoes	2 cups	500 mL
Parsley flakes	1 tsp.	5 mL
Salt	½ tsp.	2 mL
Pepper	⅛ tsp.	0.5 mL
Grated light sharp Cheddar cheese	½ cup	125 mL
Large eggs, fork-beaten	6	6

Sauté bacon in 9 to 10 inch (22 to 25 cm) non-stick frying pan for about 4 minutes until starting to brown.

Add onions. Sauté for 3 to 4 minutes until golden. Drain.

Add potato, parsley, salt and pepper. Stir until potato is heated through. Spread evenly in pan.

Sprinkle with cheese. Pour eggs over top. Cover. Cook on medium-low for about 4 minutes. Using spatula, gently move egg mixture from outer edges towards middle of pan in about 3 places, tipping pan each time to allow unset egg to run into created space. Cover. Cook for 3 to 4 minutes until set. Cover frying pan with inverted serving plate. Flip both over so frittata is on plate, browned side up, for serving. Cuts into 6 wedges.

1 wedge: 236 Calories; 15.8 g Total Fat; 467 mg Sodium; 11 g Protein; 12 g Carbohydrate; 1 g Dietary Fiber

---

Paré Pointer
All kids know the four seasons are salt, pepper, ketchup and mustard.

Potato Dumplings

A lighter version of the traditional Norwegian recipe.
Stick-to-the-ribs sustenance for those sub-zero temperatures!
Traditionally served with crisp, fried salt pork (<u>with</u> the grease!) or
melted butter drizzled over and sprinkled with salt and pepper.

Mashed potatoes	4 cups	1 L
All-purpose flour	2 cups	500 mL
Baking powder	1 tsp.	5 mL
Salt	1 tsp.	5 mL
Pepper	¼ tsp.	1 mL
Bacon slices	4	4
Bacon slices	2	2
Boiling water	8-10 qts.	8-10 L
Salt	2 tbsp.	30 mL
Bay leaf	1	1

Combine potatoes, flour, baking powder, salt and pepper in large bowl. Cover. Let stand for 15 minutes.

Cut first amount of bacon slices into 1 inch (2.5 cm) pieces. Sauté in frying pan until crisp and brown. Drain on paper towel.

Combine remaining 4 ingredients in very large stockpot or Dutch oven. Push a piece of cooked bacon into center of rounded tablespoonful (15 mL) of potato mixture. Roll in hands to seal. Continue until all dough is used. Place balls in gently simmering stock, 1 at a time, so stock keeps simmering. Simmer, uncovered, stirring occasionally, for 1 hour. Remove with slotted spoon to paper towels to drain. Makes about 32 golf ball-sized dumplings.

1 dumpling: *59 Calories; 0.5 g Total Fat; 100 mg Sodium; 2 g Protein; 12 g Carbohydrate; 1 g Dietary Fiber*

If you want potato salad but you're in a rush, peel and dice potatoes, then cook until just tender. Cool and proceed with salad. An even faster method is to use canned potatoes.

Coconut Potatoes

In Thailand this would be made with several cloves of garlic!

Peeled potatoes (about 3 medium), cut into ¼ inch (6 mm) thick slices	1½ lbs.	680 g
Water		
Cooking oil	2 tsp.	10 mL
Garlic clove, minced	1	1
Can of coconut milk	14 oz.	400 mL
Water	½ cup	125 mL
All-purpose flour	⅓ cup	75 mL
Salt	½ tsp.	2 mL
Pepper	⅛ tsp.	0.5 mL
Toasted sesame seeds	2 tbsp.	30 mL

Cook potato in first amount of water in medium saucepan until tender. Drain.

Heat cooking oil in frying pan. Add garlic. Sauté until golden. Stir in coconut milk until hot.

Gradually whisk water into flour, salt and pepper in small bowl until smooth. Stir into milk mixture until boiling and thickened. Add potato. Stir. Turn into ungreased 2 quart (2 L) casserole. Bake in 350°F (175°C) oven for 20 minutes.

Sprinkle with sesame seeds. Bake for 10 to 15 minutes until golden brown. Serves 4.

1 serving: 364 Calories; 25.2 g Total Fat; 359 mg Sodium; 6 g Protein; 33 g Carbohydrate; 5 g Dietary Fiber

Potatoes O'Brien

The pimiento not only adds to the flavor but dresses up this dish as well. No pimiento? Try the variation.

Peeled, diced potatoes	2 cups	500 mL
Chopped onion	½ cup	125 mL
Salt, sprinkle		
Pepper, sprinkle		
Cooking oil	1 tbsp.	15 mL
Jar of chopped pimiento, drained	2 oz.	57 mL

(continued on next page)

Combine first 5 ingredients in non-stick frying pan. Cook on medium-high, stirring frequently, for about 15 minutes until potato is tender and browned.

Stir in pimiento until hot. Makes 2 cups (500 mL).

1 cup (250 mL): 207 Calories; 7.2 g Total Fat; 14 mg Sodium; 4 g Protein; 33 g Carbohydrate; 3 g Dietary Fiber

Pictured on page 107.

Variation: Substitute ⅓ cup (75 mL) diced red or green pepper for pimiento.

Potato Stir-Fry

From northern China, potatoes are gently flavored with ginger. Quite distinctive.

Peeled, cubed waxy potatoes (about 3 medium)	1½ lbs.	680 g
Water		
Cornstarch	1½ tsp.	7 mL
Chicken bouillon powder	1½ tsp.	7 mL
Granulated sugar	¾ tsp.	4 mL
Salt	¾ tsp.	4 mL
Water	½ cup	125 mL
Cooking oil	1½ tbsp.	25 mL
Gingerroot slices	4-5	4-5

Cook potato in first amount of water for about 10 minutes until still firm but starting to soften. Drain.

Whisk next 5 ingredients in cup. Set aside.

Heat cooking oil in wok or frying pan. Add gingerroot. Stir-fry for about 30 seconds. Add potato. Stir-fry until heated through and starting to brown. Discard ginger slices. Stir cornstarch mixture. Stir into potato mixture until boiling and thickened. Serves 4.

1 serving: 150 Calories; 6.1 g Total Fat; 758 mg Sodium; 2 g Protein; 23 g Carbohydrate; 1 g Dietary Fiber

Side Dishes

Grated Potato Rösti

Rösti means "to cook golden and crisp." Like a large potato latke. Garnish with diced red pepper.

Unpeeled waxy potatoes (about 2 medium)	1 lb.	454 g
Water		
Finely chopped onion	⅔ cup	150 mL
Margarine (or butter)	2 tsp.	10 mL
Salt	½ tsp.	2 mL
Pepper	¹⁄₁₆ tsp.	0.5 mL
Hard margarine (or butter)	1 tbsp.	15 mL

Cook whole potatoes in boiling water in medium saucepan for 15 minutes. Drain. Cool enough to handle. Peel and coarsely grate potatoes into medium bowl.

Sauté onions in first amount of margarine in 9 to 10 inch (22 to 25 cm) non-stick frying pan until soft and clear. Add to potato. Add salt and pepper. Toss together well.

Melt ½ of second amount of margarine in same frying pan. Pack potato mixture in pan in even layer. Heat, uncovered, on medium-low for 10 to 15 minutes, pressing down occasionally with flat spatula, until golden brown on bottom. Slide out onto plate. Heat remaining margarine in pan. Invert potato onto another plate. Slide unbrowned side into frying pan. Heat on medium-low, packing down several times, for 10 to 15 minutes until browned. Cuts into 4 wedges.

1 wedge: 114 Calories; 5 g Total Fat; 400 mg Sodium; 2 g Protein; 16 g Carbohydrate; 2 g Dietary Fiber

Pictured on page 89.

Latkes

As delicious as one would expect. Attractive with lacy browned edges. See Tip, page 83, for a lower fat way to prepare.

Peeled, grated potatoes	4 cups	1 L
Medium onion, grated	1	1
Large eggs, fork-beaten	2	2
All-purpose flour	½ cup	125 mL
Salt	1½ tsp.	7 mL
Pepper	¼ tsp.	1 mL
Cooking oil	1 cup	250 mL

(continued on next page)

Squeeze and drain grated potato very well. Place in large bowl.

Add next 5 ingredients. Mix.

Heat cooking oil in large cast-iron or heavy frying pan. Drop potato mixture by ¼ cupfuls (60 mL) into pan. Flatten to 3 to 4 inch (7 to 10 cm) patty. Fry for about 3 minutes per side until golden brown and crispy. Drain on paper towels. Makes 12 latkes.

1 latke: *106 Calories; 5.6 g Total Fat; 352 mg Sodium; 3 g Protein; 12 g Carbohydrate; 1 g Dietary Fiber*

Pictured on page 89.

Boxty

An Irish dish said to have originated during the famine. Traditionally like a scone made of mashed and grated potato but fried, not baked.

Mashed potatoes	½ cup	125 mL
Peeled, grated raw potato	½ cup	125 mL
Margarine (or butter), melted	2 tbsp.	30 mL
All-purpose flour	1 cup	250 mL
Baking powder	1 tsp.	5 mL
Salt	½ tsp.	2 mL
Pepper	¹⁄₁₆ tsp.	0.5 mL
Cooking oil	2 tsp.	10 mL

Stir both potatoes and margarine in medium bowl.

Mix in flour, baking powder, salt and pepper. Turn out onto lightly floured surface. Knead gently 8 to 10 times. Form into flattened patty. Roll out to about ¼ inch (6 mm) thick. Cut into 8 wedges.

Heat cooking oil in frying pan. Add wedges. Cover. Fry on medium-low for 4 minutes per side until browned. Makes 8 wedges.

1 wedge: *127 Calories; 4 g Total Fat; 205 mg Sodium; 2 g Protein; 20 g Carbohydrate; 1 g Dietary Fiber*

 For latkes with lower fat, fry in no-stick cooking spray in non-stick pan. They will be soft, not crisp, and have the same great taste.

Side Dishes

Perogies

Tender and filling just like Baba's and stay sealed in the boiling water.

POTATO DOUGH		
All-purpose flour	2 cups	500 mL
Salt	½ tsp.	2 mL
Mashed baking potatoes (see Note)	1½ cups	375 mL
Large egg, fork-beaten	1	1
Warm water (if needed)	¼ cup	60 mL

POTATO AND ONION FILLING (enough for 1 recipe Potato Dough)		
Finely chopped onion	3 tbsp.	50 mL
Margarine (or butter), melted	3 tbsp.	50 mL
Mashed potatoes	3 cups	750 mL
Salt	¾ tsp.	4 mL
White pepper	⅛ tsp.	0.5 mL

POTATO AND CHEESE FILLING (enough for 1 recipe Potato Dough)		
Hot mashed potatoes	2 cups	500 mL
Grated sharp Cheddar cheese (or mashed creamed cottage cheese)	1⅓ cups	325 mL
Onion salt	1 tsp.	5 mL
Pepper (white is best)	¼ tsp.	1 mL

TO ASSEMBLE AND PREPARE		
Boiling water	4 qts.	4 L
Salt	1 tbsp.	15 mL
Margarine (or butter), melted (optional)		

Potato Dough: Combine flour and salt in large bowl. Make a well. Stir in mashed potato and egg. Add enough warm water to make soft dough that can be rolled. Cover with plastic wrap. Let rest for 20 minutes.

Potato And Onion Filling: Mix all 5 ingredients in medium bowl.

Potato And Cheese Filling: Mix all 4 ingredients in medium bowl.

(continued on next page)

To Assemble and Prepare: Roll ⅓ of dough to 12 inch (30 cm) circle on well-floured surface. Cover remaining dough to prevent from drying out. Cut 3 inch (7 cm) rounds. Fill each with 1 tbsp. (15 mL) filling of choice. Dampen edge. Fold over and press edges together tightly to seal. Arrange on floured cloth on flat surface. Cover with cloth to prevent dough from drying out. Repeat, re-rolling scraps of dough with next portion, until dough and filling are used up.

Boil in batches in boiling water and salt, stirring frequently, for 2 minutes until risen to surface of water and bobbed for about 1 minute. Remove with slotted spoon to bowl. To prevent sticking, lightly coat with melted margarine. Repeat until all are boiled. Makes about 4½ dozen perogies.

Food Processor Method: Combine flour and salt in food processor. Process for 10 seconds. Add mashed potato and egg. Pulse several times until moistened. Continue to process until dough starts to form a ball. Add water, a little at a time, through food chute while processing if dough seems too dry. Too much water will make dough sticky. Cover with plastic wrap. Let rest for 20 minutes.

6 perogies: 254 Calories; 5.7 g Total Fat; 428 mg Sodium; 8 g Protein; 43 g Carbohydrate; 2 g Dietary Fiber

Note: Baking potatoes are used for the dough due to their dry texture. Use for filling as well, if desired.

To Make Ahead: Lay cooked perogies in single layer on greased baking sheet. Freeze until hard. Remove to freezer plastic bag to store.

To serve perogies:
1) **Fry** frozen perogies in margarine for 5 minutes or thawed for 2 minutes.
2) **Microwave** 5 frozen perogies and 1 tsp. (5 mL) water on high (100%) for 3 minutes or thawed perogies for 1½ minutes.
3) **Boil** from frozen state for about 3 minutes until perogies float to top and are heated through.
4) **Freeze** uncooked perogies. Boil in water and salt, as above, for about 5 minutes after coming to a boil, until all are floating.

Side Dishes

Potatoes Dauphine

Fried or baked, these are fluffy and light. Pronounced doh-FEEN.

Margarine (or butter)	¼ cup	60 mL
Boiling water	½ cup	125 mL
Salt	⅛ tsp.	0.5 mL
All-purpose flour	½ cup	125 mL
Large eggs	2	2
Mashed potatoes	1 cup	250 mL

Cooking oil, for deep-frying

Heat margarine, water and salt in medium saucepan until boiling.

Add flour all at once. Stir vigorously until mixture forms a ball and leaves sides of pan. Remove from heat.

Beat in eggs, 1 at a time, until smooth and shiny. Beat in potato.

Drop heaping teaspoonfuls (5 mL) into 375°F (190°C) cooking oil. Fry for 2 minutes on each side until golden brown. To prevent splitting, don't overcook. Remove with slotted spoon to paper towels to drain. Makes about 36 balls.

1 ball: 35 Calories; 2.4 g Total Fat; 30 mg Sodium; 1 g Protein; 3 g Carbohydrate; trace Dietary Fiber

Variation: Drop potato mixture by heaping teaspoonfuls (5 mL) onto ungreased baking sheet. Bake in 425°F (220°C) oven for 20 minutes. The puffs won't be as crispy but are still light and fluffy in texture.

POTATOES DAUPHINE PARMESAN: Stir 3 tbsp. (50 mL) grated Parmesan cheese into batter with potatoes. Fry or bake as above.

Paré Pointer

That rooster is so lazy he waits for another rooster to crow and then nods his head.

Duchess Potatoes

Lots of variations make this recipe very versatile for a buffet or individual servings.

Peeled, quartered potatoes (about 4 medium)	2 lbs.	900 g
Water		
Margarine (or butter), softened	2 tbsp.	30 mL
Large eggs, fork-beaten	2	2
Seasoned salt	¼ tsp.	1 mL
Onion powder	⅛ tsp.	0.5 mL
Pepper (white is best)	⅛ tsp.	0.5 mL
Milk	¼ cup	60 mL

No-stick cooking spray (optional)

Cook potato in water in large saucepan until tender. Drain. Mash.

Mix next 6 ingredients in large bowl. Mix in potato. Using large star tip in piping bag, form into 12 swirls on greased baking sheet or spoon about ⅓ cup (75 mL) into mounds. Spike or dimple with spoon or knife.

Spray with cooking spray for crispier crust if desired. Bake in 425°F (220°C) oven for about 20 minutes until tips are golden. Makes 12 mounds.

1 mound: 97 Calories; 2.9 g Total Fat; 69 mg Sodium; 3 g Protein; 16 g Carbohydrate; 1 g Dietary Fiber

Pictured on front cover.

DUCHESS CHEESE POTATOES: Add 1 cup (250 mL) grated medium or sharp Cheddar cheese with margarine, eggs, seasonings and milk.

DUCHESS POTATO CASSEROLE: Double or triple recipe. Pack ½ into greased 2 or 3 quart (2 or 3 L) casserole. Pipe remaining ½ into swirls all over top. Bake in 350°F (175°C) oven for 25 to 30 minutes until hot.

PARMESAN DUCHESS POTATOES: Add 2 tbsp. (30 mL) grated Parmesan cheese with margarine, eggs, seasonings and milk.

MIXED DUCHESS POTATOES: Omit milk. Add ¼ cup (60 mL) sour cream and 2 tbsp. (30 mL) chopped chives.

 *When you find yourself slightly short on mashed potatoes to feed the extra person who showed up, add equal parts of potato flakes and boiling water, then mash together.*

Potato Lyonnaise

From Lyon, France and traditionally flavored with plenty of fried onions. See page 67 for an easy variation.

Unpeeled potatoes (about 4 medium)	2 lbs.	900 g
Water		
Margarine (or butter)	2 tbsp.	30 mL
Medium onions, thinly sliced	2	2
Margarine	2 tbsp.	30 mL
Salt, sprinkle		
Pepper, sprinkle		
Chopped fresh parsley	1 tbsp.	15 mL

Cook whole potatoes in water in large saucepan until tender. Drain. Cool enough to handle. Peel and cut into ¼ inch (6 mm) slices.

Heat first amount of margarine in non-stick frying pan. Add onion. Fry gently for about 15 minutes until golden. Keep warm.

Heat second amount of margarine in non-stick frying pan. Brown potato slices on both sides, sprinkling with salt and pepper. Combine with onion in serving bowl.

Sprinkle with parsley. Serves 4.

1 serving: 216 Calories; 11.9 g Total Fat; 144 mg Sodium; 3 g Protein; 26 g Carbohydrate; 3 g Dietary Fiber

1. German Potato Salad, page 39
2. Grated Potato Rösti, page 82
3. Latkes, page 82

Props Courtesy Of: La Cache
Le Gnome

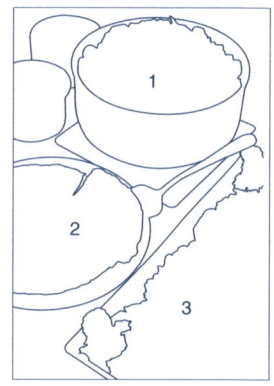

Noisettes

A novel way to serve potatoes to special guests.
They'll want to know how you made those cute, little potatoes!

Large waxy potatoes (about 2½ lbs., 1.1 kg), see Note	4	4
Cold water		
Boiling water	2 cups	500 mL
Salt	½ tsp.	2 mL
Margarine (or butter)	2 tbsp.	30 mL
Chopped fresh parsley (or ¾ tsp., 4 mL, flakes)	1 tbsp.	15 mL
Salt	½ tsp.	2 mL
Pepper, sprinkle		

Using melon baller, scoop out 1 inch (2.5 cm) balls from potatoes. Drop balls into cold water in medium saucepan. Drain.

Add boiling water and first amount of salt to saucepan. Boil for 5 minutes. Drain. Pat dry with paper towel.

Melt margarine in frying pan. Add potato. Swish around pan. Partially cover. Cook on medium for 10 to 15 minutes until tender and golden.

Sprinkle with parsley, salt and pepper. Makes about 32 balls.

5 balls: 94 Calories; 4 g Total Fat; 277 mg Sodium; 2 g Protein; 14 g Carbohydrate; 1 g Dietary Fiber

Pictured on page 107.

Note: Cook and mash leftover potato for use in another recipe.

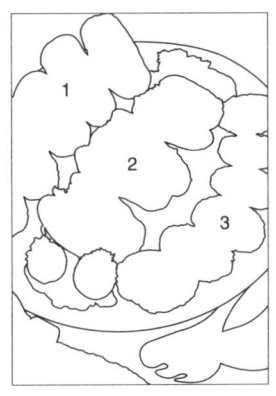

1. Potato Croquettes, page 92
2. Stuffed Green Peppers, page 99
3. Speedy Potato Patties, page 105

Props Courtesy Of: Le Gnome

Potato Croquettes

Creamy rich inside and a thick golden crust on the outside.
A very special treat! A great make-ahead.

Peeled potatoes (about 2 medium), cut up	1 lb.	454 g
Water		
Margarine (or butter)	3 tbsp.	50 mL
Finely chopped onion	¼ cup	60 mL
Finely chopped white celery	¼ cup	60 mL
All-purpose flour	7 tbsp.	115 mL
Whole milk (no substitutes)	1 cup	250 mL
Salt	¾ tsp.	4 mL
Pepper	⅛ tsp.	0.5 mL
Dill weed	½ tsp.	2 mL
Ground nutmeg, sprinkle		
Large eggs	2	2
Cold water	2 tbsp.	30 mL
Fine dry bread crumbs	1⅓ cups	325 mL

Cooking oil, for deep-frying

Cook potato in water in medium saucepan until tender. Drain. Return to heat. Gently shake to dry. Break potato into small pieces with fork, or coarsely mash.

Melt margarine in large saucepan. Add onion and celery. Sauté until very soft. Stir in flour. Slowly add milk, stirring constantly, until sauce is smooth. Heat and stir until boiling and thickened.

Stir in salt, pepper, dill and nutmeg. Mixture will be like thick glue or paste. Stir in potatoes. Turn mixture into 9 inch (22 cm) pie plate. Spread evenly. Lay plastic wrap directly on surface. Chill for several hours or overnight. Or, put into freezer for 1 hour until very cold, but not frozen. Divide into 8 wedges with knife or shape into 8 patties.

Beat eggs and second amount of water with fork in shallow dish.

(continued on next page)

Pour crumbs into separate shallow dish. Handling potato wedge carefully, put into bread crumbs. Working with crumbs, form wedge into cylinder shape. Coat completely. Roll gently in egg mixture. Coat in crumbs again. Repeat for total of 2 egg and 3 crumb coats. Chill on waxed paper for ½ hour to dry.

Deep-fry in 375°F (190°C) cooking oil for 2½ to 3 minutes, turning gently once or twice, until golden. Remove with slotted spoon to paper towels to drain. Makes 8 croquettes.

1 croquette: 251 Calories; 12.3 g Total Fat; 484 mg Sodium; 6 g Protein; 28 g Carbohydrate; 1 g Dietary Fiber

Pictured on page 90.

To Make Ahead: Cool after deep-frying. Wrap. Label and freeze. Reheat from frozen state, on baking sheet in 350°F (175°C) oven for 30 minutes.

Twice-Cooked Potatoes

A special treat that your family will love.

Unpeeled potatoes (about 4 medium), baked, see page 10	2 lbs.	900 g
Margarine (or butter)	2 tbsp.	30 mL
Salt	½ tsp.	2 mL
Pepper	⅛ tsp.	0.5 mL
Margarine (or butter)	2 tsp.	10 mL

Cut potatoes in half. Scoop out flesh into large shallow bowl. Discard skins. Add first amount of margarine, salt and pepper. Mash with fork. Form into eight 3 to 4 inch (7 to 10 cm) patties, using scant ½ cup (125 mL) for each. If potato mixture is too sticky, form patties between folded plastic wrap.

Melt 1 tsp. (5 mL) of second amount of margarine in frying pan. Add ½ of potato patties. Fry for about 4 minutes on each side until browned. Repeat with remaining margarine and patties. Makes 8 patties.

1 patty: 108 Calories; 4 g Total Fat; 219 mg Sodium; 2 g Protein; 17 g Carbohydrate; 2 g Dietary Fiber

Variation: Substitute seasoned salt in place of regular salt for a slightly different flavor.

Potato Cake

What a pretty way to serve vegetables!
Makes a conversational dish to serve company.

Margarine (or butter), 1½ tsp. (7 mL) per pan	1 tbsp.	15 mL
Fine dry bread crumbs (2 tbsp., 30 mL, per pan)	¼ cup	60 mL
Large eggs, fork-beaten	4	4
Seasoned salt	½ tsp.	2 mL
Onion salt	½ tsp.	2 mL
Lemon pepper	½ tsp.	2 mL
Parsley flakes	½ tsp.	2 mL
Mashed potatoes	3 cups	750 mL
SAUCE		
Milk	1¾ cups	425 mL
All-purpose flour	⅓ cup	75 mL
Salt	1 tsp.	5 mL
Pepper	¼ tsp.	1 mL
Onion powder	¼ tsp.	1 mL
Paprika	¼ tsp.	1 mL
Grated light sharp Cheddar cheese	1 cup	250 mL
Cooked mixed vegetables (your choice), cut bite size	3 cups	750 mL

Line two 9 inch (22 cm) round layer pans with foil. Grease foil with margarine. Coat pans heavily with bread crumbs.

Combine next 6 ingredients in medium bowl. Spread ½ of potato mixture in each pan. Bake in 400°F (205°C) oven on center rack for 30 minutes until browned. Keep warm.

Sauce: Gradually whisk milk into flour in medium saucepan until smooth. Add salt, pepper, onion powder and paprika. Heat and stir until boiling and thickened. Stir in cheese until melted.

Stir in vegetables. Heat through. Turn one potato layer onto plate. Peel off foil. Cover with ½ of vegetables. Turn out second layer on top of vegetables. Pour remaining vegetables on top. Cuts into 8 wedges.

1 wedge: 279 Calories; 9.2 g Total Fat; 789 mg Sodium; 13 g Protein; 36 g Carbohydrate; 4 g Dietary Fiber

Pictured on page 53.

(continued on next page)

Side Dishes

MEATY POTATO CAKE: Stir ¾ cup (175 mL) diced hot wieners into sauce.

BEAN POTATO CAKE: Omit cream sauce and vegetables. Spoon warm beans in tomato sauce between and on top of layers.

CHILI POTATO CAKE: Omit cream sauce and vegetables. Spoon your own warm, homemade chili between and on top of layers.

Potato Parcels

These patties have a cheese-filled center.

Peeled potatoes (about 3 medium), cut up	1½ lbs.	680 g
Water		
Milk	½ cup	125 mL
Large egg, fork-beaten	1	1
Salt	½ tsp.	2 mL
Pepper	¼ tsp.	1 mL
Onion salt	¼ tsp.	1 mL
Light sharp Cheddar cheese, cut into 12 cubes	3 oz.	85 g
TOPPING		
Margarine (or butter)	2 tbsp.	30 mL
Fine dry bread crumbs	½ cup	125 mL
Ground oregano	⅛-¼ tsp.	0.5-1 mL
Garlic powder	⅛ tsp.	0.5 mL
Onion powder	⅛ tsp.	0.5 mL

Cook potato in water in medium saucepan until tender. Drain. Mash. Add milk, egg, salt, pepper and onion salt. Mash. Form into 12 mounds on greased baking sheet.

Push 1 cheese cube into center of each. Smooth potato to cover and gently form into patty shape right on the baking sheet.

Topping: Melt margarine in small saucepan. Stir in remaining 4 ingredients. Sprinkle on patties and gently press down. Bake in 400°F (205°C) oven for 15 minutes. Makes 12 patties.

1 patty: 118 Calories; 4.2 g Total Fat; 259 mg Sodium; 4 g Protein; 16 g Carbohydrate; 1 g Dietary Fiber

Mushroom Cheese Braids

Almost too pretty to be a side dish! Could be used as a first course or appetizer as well. The traditional East Indian version of this recipe is boiled.

CRUST		
Mashed potatoes	2 cups	500 mL
Large egg	1	1
Salt	½ tsp.	2 mL
Pepper	¼ tsp.	1 mL
Grated Parmesan cheese	2 tbsp.	30 mL
All-purpose flour	1¼ cups	300 mL
FILLING		
Margarine (or butter)	1 tbsp.	15 mL
Sliced fresh mushrooms	1½ cups	375 mL
Chopped green onion	¼ cup	60 mL
Grated Gruyère cheese	1 cup	250 mL
Parsley flakes	1 tsp.	5 mL
Garlic powder (optional)	¼ tsp.	1 mL
Large egg, fork-beaten	1	1
Grated Parmesan cheese, sprinkle		

Crust: Mix all 6 ingredients in medium bowl to make soft dough. Roll out ½ on well-floured surface into 12 x 9 inch (30 x 22 cm) rectangle.

Filling: Melt margarine in frying pan. Sauté mushrooms until golden. Remove to medium bowl. Cool slightly.

Add next 4 ingredients. Stir. Spoon ½ of filling down length in center third of rectangle. Cut perpendicular slits in dough about 1 inch (2.5 cm) wide from filling outward to edges. Fold strips to cross over center portion in braid design. Repeat with second ½ of pastry and filling.

Carefully transfer braids to greased baking sheet using pancake lifter. Brush tops with egg. Sprinkle with Parmesan cheese. Bake in 375°F (190°C) oven for 25 to 30 minutes until golden brown. Cuts into 12 slices.

1 slice: 154 Calories; 5.5 g Total Fat; 191 mg Sodium; 7 g Protein; 19 g Carbohydrate; 1 g Dietary Fiber

Pictured on page 71.

Company Potatoes

A big batch of creamy, delicious potatoes for 12. Can be frozen and reheated.

Peeled potatoes (about 10 medium), cut up	5 lbs.	2.3 kg
Water		
Light cream cheese, softened	8 oz.	250 g
Light mayonnaise (or salad dressing)	1 cup	250 mL
Onion powder	1 tsp.	5 mL
Salt	1 tsp.	5 mL
Pepper	¼ tsp.	1 mL
Margarine (or butter)	1 tbsp.	15 mL

Cook potato in water in large pot or Dutch oven until tender. Drain. Mash.

Beat next 5 ingredients in small bowl until smooth. Add to potato. Mash or beat until fluffy. Turn into ungreased 3 quart (3 L) casserole. Bake in 350°F (175°C) oven for about 30 minutes until hot.

Randomly press indentations in top with bowl of spoon. Add a bit of margarine to each indentation. Makes 10 cups (2.5 L).

1 cup (250 mL): 213 Calories; 11 g Total Fat; 581 mg Sodium; 4 g Protein; 25 g Carbohydrate; 2 g Dietary Fiber

Variation: To serve immediately, heat cream cheese mixture in microwave before adding to potatoes.

GARLIC COMPANY POTATOES: Omit salt. Add 1 tsp. (5 mL) garlic salt.

Paré Pointer

When the boarding house blew up, the roomers were really flying.

Vegetables In Shells

A very pretty presentation for your next dinner party.

SHELLS		
Peeled potatoes (about 4 medium), cut up	2 lbs.	900 g
Water		
Milk	¼ cup	60 mL
Large eggs, fork-beaten	2	2
Salt	1 tsp.	5 mL
Pepper	¼ tsp.	1 mL
FILLING		
Frozen kernel corn	1 cup	250 mL
Frozen peas	1 cup	250 mL
Water		
Milk	1½ cups	375 mL
All-purpose flour	3 tbsp.	50 mL
Salt	1 tsp.	5 mL
Pepper	¼ tsp.	1 mL
Chicken bouillon powder	1 tsp.	5 mL
Paprika	¼ tsp.	1 mL

Shells: Cook potato in water in large saucepan until tender. Drain. Mash.

Mix milk, eggs, salt and pepper in small bowl. Add to potatoes. Mash well. Form mixture into 8 mounds on greased baking sheet. Use spoon to shape into shells about 1½ to 2 inches (3.8 to 5 cm) high, with ½ inch (12 mm) thick sides. Spray shells lightly with no-stick cooking spray. Bake in 375°F (190°C) oven for 30 to 40 minutes until browned.

Filling: Cook corn and peas in water in medium saucepan for 4 minutes. Drain.

Gradually stir milk into flour in separate medium saucepan until smooth.

Add salt, pepper, bouillon powder and paprika. Heat and stir until boiling and thickened. Stir in corn and peas. Heat through. Spoon into hot potato shells. Makes 8 filled shells.

1 filled shell: 144 Calories; 2 g Total Fat; 823 mg Sodium; 7 g Protein; 26 g Carbohydrate; 2 g Dietary Fiber

Pictured on front cover.

(continued on next page)

CREAMY MEAT SHELLS: Omit corn and peas. Stir 2 cups (500 mL) of finely chopped cooked ham, chicken or beef into cream sauce.

Stuffed Green Peppers

Enjoy your potatoes in an edible cup!

Large green peppers	3	3
Water		
Salt	½ tsp.	2 mL
Bacon slices, diced	5	5
Minced onion flakes	2½ tbsp.	37 mL
Peeled, cooked, diced potatoes	4 cups	1 L
Grated light sharp Cheddar cheese	1¼ cups	300 mL
Seasoned salt	¾ tsp.	4 mL
TOPPING		
Margarine (or butter), melted	1 tbsp.	15 mL
Soda cracker crumbs	¼ cup	60 mL
Grated light sharp Cheddar cheese	¼ cup	60 mL

Cut peppers in half lengthwise. Remove seeds. Boil in water and first amount of salt in large pot or Dutch oven for 3 minutes. Turn peppers, cut side down on paper towels to drain.

Cook bacon in frying pan until browned. Drain. Turn into large bowl.

Add onion, potato, cheese and seasoned salt. Stir. Fill pepper halves.

Topping: Stir margarine and cracker crumbs in small bowl. Toss with cheese. Sprinkle on potato mixture. Arrange in ungreased 2 quart (2 L) casserole. Cover. Bake in 350°F (175°C) oven for 20 minutes. Remove cover. Bake for 10 minutes until crumbs are brown. Makes 6 stuffed peppers.

1 stuffed pepper: 249 Calories; 11 g Total Fat; 514 mg Sodium; 12 g Protein; 26 g Carbohydrate; 2 g Dietary Fiber

Pictured on page 90.

Potatoes Anna

Deliciously buttery. A decadent, rich dish to serve company.

Peeled, long, narrow potatoes (about 3 medium), cut into paper-thin slices	1½ lbs.	680 g
Butter (or margarine), melted	3 tbsp.	50 mL
Salt, light sprinkle		
Pepper, light sprinkle		

Lay potato slices on part of dish towel. Fold end over and pat dry.

Grease sides and bottom of 8 inch (20 cm) round layer pan. Make 1 layer of overlapping potato slices. Brush with some of the melted butter. Make second layer, with potato slices overlapping in opposite direction. Brush with melted butter. Alternate layers of potatoes, brushing each with butter and sprinkling every second layer with salt and pepper. Repeat until potato is used. Cover with foil. Bake in 400°F (205°C) oven for 40 to 50 minutes until potatoes are soft when pierced. Invert onto serving dish to release potatoes from pan. If desired, invert onto baking sheet and brown under broiler to add more color. Serves 4.

1 serving: 144 Calories; 8.8 g Total Fat; 94 mg Sodium; 2 g Protein; 15 g Carbohydrate; 1 g Dietary Fiber

Potato Puff Balls

An attractive way to serve potatoes.

Large eggs	2	2
Onion salt	½ tsp.	2 mL
Pepper	⅛ tsp.	0.5 mL
Mashed potatoes	3 cups	750 mL
Margarine (or butter), melted	1 tbsp.	15 mL
Chopped fresh parsley (or ½ tsp., 2 mL, flakes)	2 tsp.	10 mL

(continued on next page)

Beat eggs, onion salt and pepper in medium bowl until smooth.

Add potato. Mix well. Drop by ¼ cupfuls (60 mL) onto greased baking sheet. Bake in 350°F (175°C) oven for about 10 minutes until starting to set.

Remove from oven. Drizzle each puff with melted margarine. Sprinkle with parsley. Bake for 20 minutes until puffed and lightly browned. Makes 12 puffs.

1 puff: 69 Calories; 1.8 g Total Fat; 80 mg Sodium; 2 g Protein; 12 g Carbohydrate; 1 g Dietary Fiber

Gratin Hash Browns

Short of time but still want to make your own? Try the quick variation below.

Unpeeled potatoes (about 4 medium)	2 lbs.	900 g
Water		
Margarine (or butter)	¼ cup	60 mL
Seasoned salt	¾ tsp.	4 mL
Onion powder	½ tsp.	2 mL
Pepper	¼ tsp.	1 mL
Milk	⅔ cup	150 mL
Grated light sharp Cheddar cheese	1 cup	250 mL

Cook whole potatoes in water in large saucepan for 15 to 20 minutes until just tender. Drain. Cool enough to handle. Peel. Coarsely grate potatoes into large bowl.

Melt margarine in small saucepan. Add seasoned salt, onion powder, pepper and milk. Add to potato. Add cheese. Stir very gently. Turn into shallow greased 2 quart (2 L) casserole. Bake in 350°F (175°C) oven for 1¼ to 1½ hours. Makes 5 cups (1.25 L).

1 cup (250 mL): 224 Calories; 12.6 g Total Fat; 415 mg Sodium; 8 g Protein; 20 g Carbohydrate; 1 g Dietary Fiber

Variation: Use 2.2 lb. (1 kg) bag of frozen hash brown potatoes instead of cooked grated potatoes. Increase onion powder to ¾ tsp. (4 mL) and cheese to 1½ cups (375 mL).

Con Queso Potatoes

Slight nip from chilies in a creamy, cheesy casserole.
For a pretty presentation, garnish with red chili peppers and tortilla chips.

Cans of condensed Cheddar cheese soup (10 oz., 284 mL, each)	2	2
Light sour cream	1 cup	250 mL
Finely chopped onion	½ cup	125 mL
Salsa	1 cup	250 mL
Can of diced green chilies, with liquid	4 oz.	114 mL
Salt	½ tsp.	2 mL
Pepper	⅛ tsp.	0.5 mL
Package of frozen hash brown potatoes	2.2 lbs.	1 kg
Broken up corn tortilla (or corn) chips	1½ cups	375 mL
Grated light sharp Cheddar cheese	1 cup	250 mL

Mix first 7 ingredients well in large bowl.

Stir in hash browns. Turn into greased 9 x 13 inch (22 x 33 cm) pan. Cover with foil. Bake in 350°F (175°C) oven for 45 minutes.

Sprinkle corn chips and cheese on top. Bake, uncovered, for about 15 minutes until cheese is melted. Serves 10.

1 serving: 283 Calories; 12.3 g Total Fat; 1228 mg Sodium; 10 g Protein; 35 g Carbohydrate; 3 g Dietary Fiber

Pictured on page 72.

Potato Heaps

These are so easy and they require very little attention.
Prepare the rest of your meal while they cook in the oven!

Medium onion, finely chopped	1	1
Cooking oil	2 tsp.	10 mL
Frozen hash brown potatoes	3 cups	750 mL
Chopped chives	1 tbsp.	15 mL
Salt, sprinkle		
Pepper, sprinkle		

(continued on next page)

Side Dishes

Sauté onion in cooking oil in frying pan until soft.

Mix in hash browns, chives, salt and pepper. Form into 8 heaps on greased baking sheet. Bake in 400°F (205°C) oven for 35 to 40 minutes until golden brown. Makes 8 heaps.

1 heap: 84 Calories; 1.7 g Total Fat; 19 mg Sodium; 2 g Protein; 16 g Carbohydrate; 2 g Dietary Fiber

Parmesan Hash Browns

*Little bits of orange and green throughout.
These are best served hot from the oven.*

Can of condensed cream of mushroom soup	10 oz.	284 mL
Can of skim evaporated milk	13½ oz.	385 mL
Sliced green onion	½ cup	125 mL
Grated carrot	1 cup	250 mL
Grated Parmesan cheese	½ cup	125 mL
Pepper	¼ tsp.	1 mL
Package of frozen hash brown potatoes	2.2 lbs.	1 kg
Can of french-fried onion rings	2¾ oz.	79 g

Mix first 6 ingredients well in large bowl.

Add hash browns. Stir. Turn into greased 9 x 13 inch (22 x 33 cm) pan. Bake in 350°F (175°C) oven for about 50 minutes.

Cover with onion rings. Bake for 10 minutes to heat through. Serves 12.

1 serving: 172 Calories; 5.1 g Total Fat; 384 mg Sodium; 7 g Protein; 25 g Carbohydrate; 2 g Dietary Fiber

If you or someone in your household regularly peels potatoes or sweet potatoes quite thick, deep-fry the peels for a crispy treat.

Mashed Ricotta Potatoes

Crunchy, toasted almonds complement the mild flavor and add some interest to otherwise white potatoes.

Peeled potatoes (about 4 medium), cut up	2 lbs.	900 g
Medium onion, coarsely chopped	1	1
Water		
Part-skim ricotta (or creamed cottage) cheese	2 cups	500 mL
Light sour cream	½ cup	125 mL
Salt	½ tsp.	2 mL
Pepper	⅛ tsp.	0.5 mL
Sliced almonds, toasted	¼ cup	60 mL

Cook potato and onion in water in large saucepan until tender. Drain. Mash very well.

Add cheese, sour cream, salt and pepper. Stir. Turn into ungreased 2 quart (2 L) casserole.

Sprinkle with almonds. Bake in 350°F (175°C) oven for about 30 minutes until heated through. Makes 6 cups (1.5 L).

1 cup (250 mL): 185 Calories; 7.9 g Total Fat; 261 mg Sodium; 10 g Protein; 20 g Carbohydrate; 2 g Dietary Fiber

Speedy Cheesy Potatoes

Little green bits of chives show through to make these interesting. Easy to double for company.

Peeled potatoes (about 3 medium), cut up	1½ lbs.	680 g
Water		
Light cream cheese, softened	4 oz.	125 g
Onion powder	¼ tsp.	1 mL
Salt	½ tsp.	2 mL
Pepper	⅛ tsp.	0.5 mL
Chopped chives	2 tsp.	10 mL
Milk	½ cup	125 mL

(continued on next page)

Cook potato in water in medium saucepan until tender. Drain. Mash.

Combine next 5 ingredients in small bowl. Beat in milk, a little at a time. Heat in microwave until hot. Add to potato. Mash. Makes 3 cups (750 mL).

1 cup (250 mL): 166 Calories; 5.7 g Total Fat; 658 mg Sodium; 6 g Protein; 23 g Carbohydrate; 1 g Dietary Fiber

Speedy Potato Patties

Frying patties in cooking oil produces a crispier crust but lightly spraying a non-stick pan will work almost as well. A nice blend of spices make these extra delicious besides being speedy!

Water	1 cup	250 mL
Large egg	1	1
Chopped fresh parsley (or ¼ tsp., 1 mL, flakes)	1½ tbsp.	25 mL
Salt	¼ tsp.	1 mL
Onion powder	¼ tsp.	1 mL
Dried sweet basil	⅛ tsp.	0.5 mL
Dried whole oregano	⅛ tsp.	0.5 mL
Ground rosemary	1/16 tsp.	0.5 mL
Fine dry bread crumbs	½ cup	125 mL
Instant potato flakes	1 cup	250 mL
Grated light sharp Cheddar cheese	½ cup	125 mL
Cooking oil (optional)	2 tsp.	10 mL

Beat first 8 ingredients with fork in medium bowl.

Add bread crumbs, potato flakes and cheese. Stir well. Let stand until slightly firm. Shape into patties using ¼ cup (60 mL) dry measure. Mixture will be slightly sticky.

Fry patties in cooking oil in non-stick pan for 2 to 3 minutes on each side until browned. Makes 8 patties.

1 patty: 79 Calories; 3.1 g Total Fat; 176 mg Sodium; 4 g Protein; 9 g Carbohydrate; 1 g Dietary Fiber

Pictured on page 90.

Browned Onion With Potatoes

Caramelized onions give a boost to plain mashed potatoes.

Peeled potatoes (about 4 medium), cut up	2 lbs.	900 g
Water		
Medium onions, cut into thin slices	2	2
Margarine (or butter)	1 tbsp.	15 mL
Hot milk	⅓ cup	75 mL
Margarine (or butter)	1 tbsp.	15 mL
Salt	½ tsp.	2 mL
Pepper	⅛ tsp.	0.5 mL

Cook potato in water in large saucepan until tender. Drain. Mash.

Sauté onion in first amount of margarine in frying pan until medium to dark brown.

Add remaining 4 ingredients to potato. Mash well. Stir in onion. Makes 4 cups (1 L).

1 cup (250 mL): 199 Calories; 6.3 g Total Fat; 427 mg Sodium; 4 g Protein; 33 g Carbohydrate; 3 g Dietary Fiber

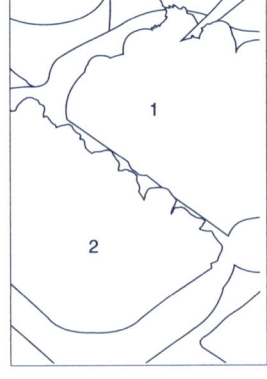

1. Noisettes, page 91
2. Potatoes O'Brien, page 80

Props Courtesy Of: Le Gnome

Deluxe Potatoes

Creamy and moist mashed potatoes.
Larger quantity is perfect to make ahead for company.

Peeled potatoes (about 10 medium), cut up	5 lbs.	2.3 kg
Water		
Light cream cheese, softened	8 oz.	250 g
Light sour cream	1 cup	250 mL
Margarine (or butter)	2 tbsp.	30 mL
Seasoned salt	2 tsp.	10 mL
Pepper	¼ tsp.	1 mL

Cook potato in water in large saucepan until tender. Drain. Mash.

Beat next 5 ingredients in small bowl until smooth. Heat in microwave on high (100%) for 2 minutes. Add to potato. Mash well. Turn into greased 9 x 13 inch (22 x 33 cm) pan. Cover with foil. Bake in 350°F (175°C) oven for about 30 minutes until hot. Makes 10 cups (2.5 L).

1 cup (250 mL): 211 Calories; 8.4 g Total Fat; 554 mg Sodium; 6 g Protein; 29 g Carbohydrate; 2 g Dietary Fiber

To Make Ahead: Cover and chill for up to 2 days. To serve, cover with foil. Bake in 350°F (175°C) oven for 45 to 60 minutes until heated through.

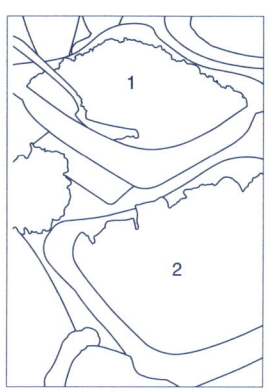

1. Heaven And Earth, page 112
2. Italian Potato Roast, page 119

Side Dishes

Colcannon

Good texture and flavor. Eat your vegetables and potatoes in one dish. An Irish favorite with or without parsnips and onions.

Peeled potatoes (about 5 medium), cut up	2½ lbs.	1.1 kg
Peeled medium parsnips, cut up	2	2
Medium onions, chopped	2	2
Shredded cabbage, lightly packed	2 cups	500 mL
Water		
Margarine (or butter)	¼ cup	60 mL
Salt	1 tsp.	5 mL
Pepper	¼ tsp.	1 mL

Cook first 5 ingredients in large saucepan until vegetables are tender. Drain. Mash.

Add margarine, salt and pepper. Mash until margarine is melted. Makes 6 cups (1.5 L).

1 cup (250 mL): 211 Calories; 8.5 g Total Fat; 562 mg Sodium; 3 g Protein; 32 g Carbohydrate; 4 g Dietary Fiber

Garlic Mashed Potatoes

Good, mellow garlic flavor.

Peeled potatoes (about 4 medium), cut up	2 lbs.	900 g
Water		
Garlic cloves, minced	3	3
Margarine (or butter)	1 tbsp.	15 mL
Skim evaporated milk, heated	⅔ cup	150 mL
Salt	1 tsp.	5 mL
Pepper	⅛ tsp.	0.5 mL

Cook potato in water in large saucepan until tender. Drain. Mash.

Sauté garlic in margarine in small frying pan until softened. Add to potato. Stir.

Add milk, salt and pepper. Mash well. Makes about 5 cups (1.25 L).

1 cup (250 mL): 121 Calories; 2.1 g Total Fat; 515 mg Sodium; 4 g Protein; 22 g Carbohydrate; 1 g Dietary Fiber

Chantilly Potatoes

Mild cheese flavor in melt-in-your-mouth soft potatoes. Delicious!

Peeled potatoes (about 4 medium), cut up	2 lbs.	900 g
Water		
Milk	½ cup	125 mL
Salt	¾ tsp.	4 mL
Pepper	¼ tsp.	1 mL
Grated light sharp Cheddar cheese	½ cup	125 mL
Whipping cream	½ cup	125 mL
Onion salt	⅛ tsp.	0.5 mL

Cook potato in water in large saucepan until tender. Drain. Mash.

Add milk, salt, pepper and cheese. Mash well. Spread in greased 9 x 9 inch (22 x 22 cm) pan or shallow 1½ quart (1.5 L) casserole.

Beat whipping cream and onion salt in small bowl until cream is stiff. Spread on potato. Bake in 400°F (205°C) oven for about 20 minutes until golden brown. Serves 6.

1 serving: 181 Calories; 9.1 g Total Fat; 453 mg Sodium; 5 g Protein; 20 g Carbohydrate; 1 g Dietary Fiber

Creamy Potatoes

A delicate hint of savory herb makes these just a touch different.

Peeled potatoes (about 4 medium), cut up	2 lbs.	900 g
Water		
Light sour cream	½ cup	125 mL
Margarine (or butter)	1 tbsp.	15 mL
Salt	½ tsp.	2 mL
Pepper	⅛ tsp.	0.5 mL
Ground savory	⅛ tsp.	0.5 mL

Cook potato in water in medium saucepan until tender. Drain. Mash.

Add remaining 5 ingredients. Mash well. Makes 4 cups (1 L).

1 cup (250 mL): 113 Calories; 3.5 g Total Fat; 262 mg Sodium; 2 g Protein; 19 g Carbohydrate; 1 g Dietary Fiber

Heaven And Earth

How can you not love that delicious bacon and onion flavor?!
To dress up this German dish, garnish with red apple slices and bacon.

Peeled, cubed potatoes (about 4 medium)	2 lbs.	900 g
Water		
Salt	1 tsp.	5 mL
Peeled, sliced medium cooking apples (such as McIntosh)	5-6	5-6
Bacon slices, diced	8	8
Medium onion, chopped	1	1

Cook potato in water and salt in large saucepan until tender-crisp.

Add apple. Cook until both apple and potato are tender. Drain. Keep hot.

Sauté bacon in frying pan for about 4 minutes until starting to brown.

Stir in onion. Sauté until bacon and onion are browned. Drain well. Coarsely mash potato and apple. Stir in ¾ of bacon-onion mixture. Turn into serving bowl. Sprinkle with remaining bacon and onion. Makes 5 cups (1.25 L).

1 cup (250 mL): 194 Calories; 4.6 g Total Fat; 140 mg Sodium; 4 g Protein; 36 g Carbohydrate; 4 g Dietary Fiber

Pictured on page 108.

Potato Puff Casserole

Has a wonderful texture. Do not freeze.

Large eggs	2	2
Mashed potatoes	2 cups	500 mL
Hard margarine (or butter), melted	2 tbsp.	30 mL
Milk	½ cup	125 mL
Grated medium Cheddar cheese	½ cup	125 mL
Seasoned salt	½ tsp.	2 mL
Onion powder	¼ tsp.	1 mL

(continued on next page)

Beat eggs in medium bowl until smooth. Add potatoes, margarine and milk. Beat to mix. Stir in cheese, seasoned salt and onion powder. Turn into greased 1 quart (1 L) casserole. Bake in 350°F (175°C) oven for 50 to 55 minutes until puffed and lightly browned. Makes 2½ cups (625 mL).

1 cup (250 mL): 257 Calories; 13.3 g Total Fat; 378 mg Sodium; 10 g Protein; 25 g Carbohydrate; 2 g Dietary Fiber

Creamy Spinach Potatoes

A delicious way to serve vegetables.
Decorate with fresh spinach leaves and lemon zest if desired.

Peeled potatoes (about 3 medium), cut up	1½ lbs.	680 g
Water		
Margarine (or butter)	2 tbsp.	30 mL
All-purpose flour	¼ cup	60 mL
Milk	2 cups	500 mL
Onion salt	½ tsp.	2 mL
Salt	½ tsp.	2 mL
Pepper	⅛ tsp.	0.5 mL
Garlic powder (optional)	¼ tsp.	1 mL
Frozen chopped spinach, thawed and squeezed dry	10 oz.	300 g
Grated Parmesan cheese	1 tbsp.	15 mL

Cook potato in water in medium saucepan until tender. Drain. Coarsely mash.

Melt margarine in medium saucepan. Stir in flour until smooth. Slowly whisk in milk. Add next 4 ingredients. Heat and stir until boiling and thickened.

Stir in spinach. Turn potato into greased 2 quart (2 L) baking dish. Pour sauce on top. Poke randomly with spoon to allow some sauce down into potato.

Sprinkle with Parmesan cheese. Bake in 350°F (175°C) oven for 30 minutes until hot. Serves 6.

1 serving: 165 Calories; 5.4 g Total Fat; 482 mg Sodium; 6 g Protein; 24 g Carbohydrate; 2 g Dietary Fiber

Pictured on page 126.

Potatoes With Mushrooms

Something just a bit different.

Peeled potatoes (about 4 medium), cut up	2 lbs.	900 g
Water		
Tiny whole fresh mushrooms, halved or left whole	2 cups	500 mL
Margarine (or butter)	1 tbsp.	15 mL
Skim evaporated milk	½ cup	125 mL
Milk	¼ cup	60 mL
Green onions, sliced	2	2
Salt	½ tsp.	2 mL
Pepper	⅛ tsp.	0.5 mL
Dried thyme	1/16 tsp.	0.5 mL

Cook potato in water in large saucepan until tender. Drain. Mash.

Sauté mushrooms in margarine in frying pan until golden. Add to potato.

Add next 6 ingredients. Stir well. Turn into greased 1½ quart (1.5 L) casserole. Bake, uncovered, in 375°F (190°C) oven for about 25 minutes until browned and hot. Makes 4 cups (1 L).

1 cup (250 mL): 124 Calories; 2.3 g Total Fat; 286 mg Sodium; 4 g Protein; 22 g Carbohydrate; 2 g Dietary Fiber

Horseradish Potatoes

Mashed potatoes with an extra touch. Very complementary with roast beef.

Peeled potatoes (about 6 medium), cut up	3 lbs.	1.4 kg
Water		
Salt	½ tsp.	2 mL
Margarine (or butter)	¼ cup	60 mL
Onion powder	¼ tsp.	1 mL
White pepper	⅛ tsp.	0.5 mL
Skim evaporated milk, heated	½ cup	125 mL
Creamed horseradish	1-2 tbsp.	15-30 mL

(continued on next page)

Cook potato in water and salt in large saucepan until tender. Drain. Mash.

Add remaining 5 ingredients. Mash until margarine is melted. Makes 6 cups (1.5 L).

1 cup (250 mL): 156 Calories; 6.3 g Total Fat; 99 mg Sodium; 3 g Protein; 23 g Carbohydrate; 1 g Dietary Fiber

Double Cheese Potatoes

Very creamy and moist. Good make-ahead dish.

Peeled potatoes (about 8 medium), cut up	4 lbs.	1.8 kg
Water		
Light cream cheese, softened	8 oz.	250 g
Light sour cream	1 cup	250 mL
Milk	½ cup	125 mL
Onion salt	1 tbsp.	15 mL
Pepper	¼ tsp.	1 mL
Grated sharp Cheddar cheese	¾ cup	175 mL

Cook potato in water in large uncovered pot or Dutch oven until tender. Drain. Mash.

Beat cream cheese and sour cream in medium microwave-safe bowl until smooth. Add milk, onion salt and pepper. Beat well. Heat in microwave on high (100%) until hot. Add to potato. Mash well.

Stir in Cheddar cheese. Makes 8 cups (2 L).

1 cup (250 mL): 261 Calories; 11.4 g Total Fat; 832 mg Sodium; 10 g Protein; 31 g Carbohydrate; 2 g Dietary Fiber

EXTRA CHEESY POTATOES: Sprinkle an additional 1 cup (250 mL) Cheddar cheese on top of casserole. Bake, uncovered, in 350°F (175°C) oven for 1 to 1½ hours until hot.

To Make Ahead: Put potato mixture into 3 quart (3 L) covered casserole. Chill for up to 2 days. Do not freeze. Bake, covered, in 350°F (175°C) oven for about 1 hour until hot.

Potato Parmesan Roast

Noticeable onion and Parmesan cheese flavor.

Peeled, cubed potatoes	2 cups	500 mL
Margarine (or butter), melted	1 tbsp.	15 mL
Grated Parmesan cheese	⅓ cup	75 mL
Parsley flakes	½ tsp.	2 mL
Garlic powder (optional)	⅛ tsp.	0.5 mL
Salt	¼ tsp.	1 mL
Pepper	⅛ tsp.	0.5 mL
Medium onion, sliced	1	1
Peeled, cubed potatoes	2 cups	500 mL
Margarine (or butter), melted	1 tbsp.	15 mL

Toss first amounts of potato and margarine in large bowl. Turn into ungreased 2 quart (2 L) casserole.

Mix next 5 ingredients in small cup. Sprinkle ½ on top of potatoes.

Layer onion on top.

Toss second amounts of potato and margarine in large bowl. Add to casserole. Sprinkle with remaining Parmesan mixture. Bake, uncovered, in 400°F (205°C) oven for 55 to 60 minutes until potato is tender. Makes 5 cups (1.25 L).

1 cup (250 mL): 157 Calories; 5.5 g Total Fat; 270 mg Sodium; 5 g Protein; 23 g Carbohydrate; 2 g Dietary Fiber

Rapid growth or sudden temperature change may cause "hollowheart," a discolored cavity in a potato. Cut out the affected area and the rest is fine to eat.

Oven Fries

Good fry taste without deep-frying.

Peeled potatoes (about 4 medium), cut into narrow fingers	2 lbs.	900 g
Cooking oil	1 tbsp.	15 mL
Salt	½ tsp.	2 mL
Pepper, sprinkle		

Combine potato and cooking oil in large bowl. Toss gently to coat well. Spread on greased baking sheet. Bake in 450°F (230°C) oven for 40 to 45 minutes, turning once or twice, until tender.

Sprinkle with salt and pepper. Serves 4.

1 serving: 119 Calories; 3.6 g Total Fat; 346 mg Sodium; 2 g Protein; 20 g Carbohydrate; 2 g Dietary Fiber

CHEESE FRIES: Sprinkle baked fries with 1 to 2 tbsp. (15 to 30 mL) grated Parmesan cheese when seasoning with salt and pepper.

CHILI FRIES: Toss potato with ½ tsp. (2 mL) chili powder before baking.

Gold Roast Potatoes

Seasoned golden potatoes.

Peeled potatoes (about 6 medium), cut in half lengthwise	3 lbs.	1.4 kg
Cooking oil (or melted margarine or butter)	2 tbsp.	30 mL
Seasoned salt	½ tsp.	2 mL
Salt	⅛ tsp.	0.5 mL
Pepper, sprinkle		

Blot potatoes dry with paper towel.

Brush potatoes with ½ of cooking oil. Arrange, cut side down, in greased 9 × 13 inch (22 × 33 cm) pan. Sprinkle with ½ of seasoned salt, salt and pepper. Cover with foil. Bake in 400°F (205°C) oven for 25 minutes. Turn potatoes over. Brush with remaining cooking oil. Sprinkle with remaining seasoned salt, salt and pepper. Bake, uncovered, for 35 to 40 minutes until tender and golden brown. Serves 6.

1 serving: 129 Calories; 4.7 g Total Fat; 179 mg Sodium; 2 g Protein; 20 g Carbohydrate; 2 g Dietary Fiber

Baked Fries

Great flavor boost to commercial french fries.

Package of frozen french fries	2.2 lbs.	1 kg
Salt, sprinkle		
Pepper, sprinkle		
Grated Parmesan cheese (or powdered Cheddar cheese product)	¼ cup	60 mL

Arrange potatoes in single layer on greased baking sheet. Bake in 450°F (230°C) oven for 15 minutes or as directed on package.

Sprinkle with salt and pepper. Sprinkle with Parmesan cheese. Toss to coat. Serves 6.

1 serving: 390 Calories; 15.9 g Total Fat; 134 mg Sodium; 8 g Protein; 57 g Carbohydrate; 5 g Dietary Fiber

Potato Crunchies

Crunchy outside and creamy inside with a toasted cereal flavor.

Mashed potatoes	2 cups	500 mL
Salt (optional)	½ tsp.	2 mL
Pepper	⅛ tsp.	0.5 mL
Margarine (or butter)	2 tbsp.	30 mL
Crushed corn flakes (or crisp rice) cereal	1 cup	250 mL

Mix potato, salt and pepper in medium bowl. Shape into eight 1½ inch (3.8 cm) balls using scant ¼ cup (60 mL) for each.

Melt margarine in small saucepan. Roll each ball in margarine with fork to coat.

Put cereal into medium bowl. Roll each potato ball in cereal to coat. Transfer to ungreased baking sheet. Bake in 350°F (175°C) oven for 15 to 20 minutes until hot and browned. Makes 8 balls.

1 ball: 110 Calories; 3 g Total Fat; 129 mg Sodium; 2 g Protein; 20 g Carbohydrate; 1 g Dietary Fiber

Italian Potato Roast

You can't get any easier than this! To add a dash of color, garnish with parsley.

Unpeeled potatoes (about 5 medium), cut into chunks	2½ lbs.	1.1 kg
Olive oil	2 tbsp.	30 mL
Package of Zesty Italian dressing mix	¾ oz.	21 g

Put potato chunks into large sealable plastic bag. Drizzle olive oil inside. Seal bag. Shake to coat potatoes.

Sprinkle dressing mix into bag. Seal. Shake well to coat potatoes. Arrange potatoes in single layer on greased baking sheet. Bake in 400°F (205°C) oven for 30 minutes. Stir. Bake for 5 to 10 minutes until browned and tender. Serves 4.

1 serving: 156 Calories; 7 g Total Fat; 493 mg Sodium; 3 g Protein; 22 g Carbohydrate; 2 g Dietary Fiber

Pictured on page 108.

Quick Cheese Potatoes

Mild cheese flavor and an attractive peach color.

Peeled potatoes (about 5 medium), cut up	1½ lbs.	680 g
Water		
Hot milk	¾ cup	175 mL
Salt	1 tsp.	5 mL
Pepper	⅛ tsp.	0.5 mL
Powdered Cheddar cheese product, sieved (or process cheese spread)	¼ cup	60 mL

Cook potato in water in large saucepan until tender. Drain. Mash.

Add milk, salt, pepper and cheese. Mash well. Makes 3 cups (750 mL).

1 cup (250 mL): 129 Calories; 2.2 g Total Fat; 830 mg Sodium; 5 g Protein; 23 g Carbohydrate; 1 g Dietary Fiber

Full O' Beans Spud

Bite into these overstuffed potatoes and find the colorful surprises inside!

Large potatoes, baked (see page 10)	3	3
Milk	⅓ cup	75 mL
Seasoned salt	¾ tsp.	4 mL
Kidney beans, drained	¾ cup	175 mL
Seeded, diced medium tomato	1	1
Grated light sharp Cheddar cheese	½ cup	125 mL
Green onion, chopped	1	1
Grated light sharp Cheddar cheese	⅓ cup	75 mL

Cut potatoes in half lengthwise. Scoop out pulp into medium bowl, leaving shells ¼ inch (6 mm) thick. Mash potato pulp.

Add milk and seasoned salt. Mash well.

Put about 1 tbsp. (15 mL) potato mixture into each shell bottom. Layer beans, tomato and first amount of cheese, dividing among shells. Dampen hands to mound and pack remaining potato on top.

Top with onion and second amount of cheese. Arrange on ungreased baking sheet. Bake in 350°F (175°C) oven for 20 minutes until heated through. Makes 6 stuffed potatoes.

1 stuffed potato: 199 Calories; 3.8 g Total Fat; 347 mg Sodium; 9 g Protein; 33 g Carbohydrate; 4 g Dietary Fiber

Cheese-Stuffed Potatoes

Two cheeses to tantalize and satisfy.

Medium potatoes, baked (see page 10)	4	4
Milk	¼ cup	60 mL
Onion salt	¼ tsp.	1 mL
Pepper	¹⁄₁₆ tsp.	0.5 mL
Grated Havarti (or Dofino) cheese	¾ cup	175 mL
Grated Parmesan cheese	4 tsp.	20 mL

(continued on next page)

Cut ¼ inch (6 mm) lengthwise from top of each potato. Scoop out pulp into medium bowl, leaving shells about ¼ inch (6 mm) thick. Discard tops once pulp is removed. Mash potato pulp.

Add milk, onion salt and pepper. Mash well.

Add Havarti cheese. Mash. Stuff shells.

Sprinkle with Parmesan cheese. Arrange on ungreased baking sheet. Bake in 350°F (175°C) oven for 20 minutes until heated through. Makes 4 stuffed potatoes.

1 stuffed potato: 258 Calories; 6.8 g Total Fat; 317 mg Sodium; 10 g Protein; 40 g Carbohydrate; 3 g Dietary Fiber

Broccoli-Stuffed Potatoes

Lots of tender-crisp broccoli and cheese. Yummy comfort food.

Large potatoes, baked (see page 10)	2	2
Frozen chopped broccoli	2 cups	500 mL
Water	½ cup	125 mL
Milk	½ cup	125 mL
Salt	½ tsp.	2 mL
Pepper	¹⁄₁₆ tsp.	0.5 mL
Grated light sharp Cheddar cheese	1 cup	250 mL
Grated light sharp Cheddar cheese	¼ cup	60 mL

Cut potatoes in half lengthwise. Scoop out pulp into medium bowl, leaving shells ¼ inch (6 mm) thick. Mash potato pulp.

Cook broccoli in water in medium saucepan until tender-crisp. Drain well. Chop into smaller pieces.

Add milk, salt and pepper to potato. Mash well.

Add first amount of cheese. Mash. Stir in broccoli. Stuff shells.

Sprinkle with second amount of cheese. Arrange on ungreased baking sheet. Bake in 350°F (175°C) oven for 20 minutes until heated through. Makes 4 stuffed potatoes.

1 stuffed potato: 264 Calories; 8 g Total Fat; 626 mg Sodium; 16 g Protein; 33 g Carbohydrate; 6 g Dietary Fiber

Reuben-Stuffed Potatoes

Sauerkraut is mellowed by potato. Serve with salad for a complete meal.

Large potatoes, baked (see page 10)	4	4
Milk	¼ cup	60 mL
Pepper	1/16 tsp.	0.5 mL
Sauerkraut, rinsed and drained	1 cup	250 mL
Chopped corned beef	1 cup	250 mL
Grated Swiss (or mozzarella) cheese	1 cup	250 mL

Cut potatoes in half lengthwise. Scoop out pulp into medium bowl, leaving shells about ¼ inch (6 mm) thick. Mash potato pulp.

Add milk and pepper. Mash.

Add sauerkraut and corned beef. Mix well. Stuff shells.

Top with cheese. Arrange on ungreased baking sheet. Bake in 350°F (175°C) oven for 20 minutes until heated through. Makes 8 stuffed potatoes.

1 stuffed potato: 220 Calories; 7.7 g Total Fat; 406 mg Sodium; 10 g Protein; 28 g Carbohydrate; 3 g Dietary Fiber

Pictured on page 125.

Sour Cream-Stuffed Potatoes

Have these on hand in the freezer to reheat anytime you want that simple, baked potato flavor.

Medium potatoes, baked (see page 10)	4	4
Light sour cream	½ cup	125 mL
Margarine (or butter)	¼ cup	60 mL
Green onion, thinly sliced	1	1
Garlic powder, sprinkle (optional)		
Salt	1/16 tsp.	0.5 mL
Pepper	1/16 tsp.	0.5 mL

(continued on next page)

Cut ¼ inch (6 mm) lengthwise from top of each potato. Scoop out pulp into medium bowl, leaving potato shells about ¼ inch (6 mm) thick. Discard tops once pulp is removed. Mash potato pulp.

Add remaining 6 ingredients. Mash well. Stuff shells. Arrange on ungreased baking sheet. Bake in 350°F (175°C) oven for 20 minutes until heated through. Serves 4.

1 serving: 303 Calories; 14.6 g Total Fat; 211 mg Sodium; 5 g Protein; 40 g Carbohydrate; 3 g Dietary Fiber

Kids' Stuffed Spuds

(Say that 5 times real fast!) Your kids will love these full-meal potatoes!

Large potatoes, baked (see page 10)	2	2
Chopped onion	¾ cup	175 mL
Margarine (or butter)	1 tbsp.	15 mL
Light salad dressing (or mayonnaise)	½ cup	125 mL
Prepared mustard	½-1 tbsp.	7-15 mL
Salt, sprinkle		
Pepper, sprinkle		
Sweet pickle relish	¼ cup	60 mL
Wieners, chopped	2	2
Ketchup (optional)		

Cut potatoes in half lengthwise. Scoop out pulp into medium bowl, leaving shells ¼ inch (6 mm) thick. Mash potato pulp.

Sauté onion in margarine in frying pan until golden.

Add salad dressing, mustard, salt and pepper to potato pulp. Mash well.

Stir in onion, relish and wieners. Stuff shells.

Squeeze zigzag line of ketchup across top. Arrange on ungreased baking sheet. Bake in 350°F (175°C) oven for 20 minutes until heated through. Makes 4 stuffed potatoes.

1 stuffed potato: 312 Calories; 16.6 g Total Fat; 584 mg Sodium; 5 g Protein; 37 g Carbohydrate; 3 g Dietary Fiber

Bacon And Cheese Spuds

Super decadent stuffing. A real filler upper!

Medium potatoes, baked (see page 10)	4	4
Herb-flavored non-fat spreadable cream cheese	¼ cup	60 mL
Milk	1 tbsp.	15 mL
Grated light sharp Cheddar cheese	¼ cup	60 mL
Salt	¼ tsp.	1 mL
Pepper	1/16 tsp.	0.5 mL
Bacon slices, diced	3	3
Chopped fresh mushrooms	½ cup	125 mL
Chopped green onion	2 tbsp.	30 mL
Grated light sharp Cheddar cheese	¼ cup	60 mL

Cut ¼ inch (6 mm) lengthwise from top of each potato. Scoop out pulp into medium bowl, leaving shells ¼ inch (6 mm) thick. Discard tops once pulp is removed. Mash pulp.

Add next 5 ingredients. Beat until smooth.

Fry bacon in frying pan for 3 to 4 minutes until crisp. Remove bacon with slotted spoon. Add to potato pulp, reserving about 1 tbsp. (15 mL) for garnish.

Drain all but 1 tsp. (5 mL) fat from frying pan. Add mushrooms and green onion. Sauté until soft. Mix with potato pulp. Stuff shells.

Arrange on ungreased baking sheet. Sprinkle with second amount of Cheddar cheese. Sprinkle with reserved bacon. Bake in 350°F (175°C) oven for 20 minutes until heated through. Makes 4 stuffed potatoes.

1 stuffed potato: 257 Calories; 5.6 g Total Fat; 357 mg Sodium; 10 g Protein; 42 g Carbohydrate; 4 g Dietary Fiber

Pictured on page 125.

1. Reuben-Stuffed Potatoes, page 122
2. Cranberry Hasselback Yams, page 129
3. Bacon and Cheese Spuds, above

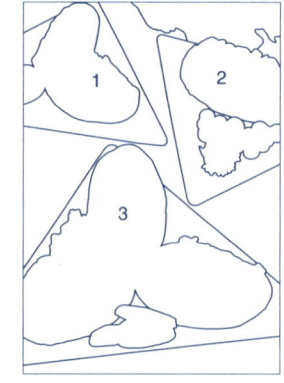

Sweet Potato Bake

Delicate orange flavor.

Cans of sweet potatoes (19 oz., 540 mL, each), drained, or 3 cups (750 mL) fresh, boiled and coarsely mashed	2	2
Large eggs	2	2
Grated orange peel	1½ tsp.	7 mL
Freshly squeezed orange juice	3 tbsp.	50 mL
Granulated sugar	2 tbsp.	30 mL
Vanilla	1 tsp.	5 mL
Salt	¼ tsp.	1 mL
Margarine (or butter)	3 tbsp.	50 mL
Brown sugar, packed	½ cup	125 mL
All-purpose flour	¼ cup	60 mL

Stir first 7 ingredients in medium bowl. Turn into ungreased shallow 2 quart (2 L) casserole.

Melt margarine in small saucepan. Stir in sugar and flour. Sprinkle on top. Bake, uncovered, in 350°F (175°C) oven for 45 minutes until hot and set. Serves 6.

1 serving: 331 Calories; 7.9 g Total Fat; 290 mg Sodium; 5 g Protein; 61 g Carbohydrate; 4 g Dietary Fiber

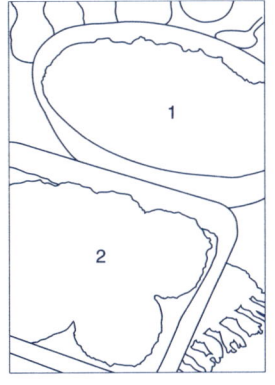

1. Creamy Spinach Potatoes, page 113
2. Rum-Sauced Patties, page 128

Props Courtesy Of: Le Gnome
                    The Bay

Sweet Potato Patties

Serve these with light sour cream.

Peeled, grated raw sweet potatoes	2 cups	500 mL
All-purpose flour	¼ cup	60 mL
Granulated sugar	¼ cup	60 mL
Salt	¼ tsp.	1 mL
Cooking oil	2 tbsp.	30 mL

Mix first 4 ingredients well in medium bowl. Use ¼ cup (60 mL) measure to shape into eight 3 inch (7 cm) circles about ¼ inch (6 mm) thick.

Heat 1 tbsp. (15 mL) cooking oil in large non-stick frying pan on medium-low. Fry ½ of patties for 3 to 4 minutes per side until browned. Drain on paper towels. Repeat with remaining cooking oil and patties. Makes 8 patties.

1 patty: 113 Calories; 3.6 g Total Fat; 90 mg Sodium; 1 g Protein; 19 g Carbohydrate; 1 g Dietary Fiber

Rum-Sauced Patties

Plenty of thick, caramel-like sauce that can also be spooned onto ham steaks or barbecued pork chops.

Sweet potato patties, see above

Brown sugar, packed	½ cup	125 mL
All-purpose flour	3 tbsp.	50 mL
Prepared orange juice	½ cup	125 mL
Water	½ cup	125 mL
Rum flavoring	1 tsp.	5 mL

Layer browned patties in ungreased shallow 2 quart (2 L) casserole.

Mix brown sugar and flour well in small saucepan. Stir in orange juice until smooth. Add water and rum flavoring. Heat and stir until boiling. Pour over patties. Bake, uncovered, at 350°F (175°C) for about 20 minutes until heated through and bubbling. Makes 8 small patties and 1½ cups (375 mL) sauce.

1 patty and 3 tbsp. (50 mL) sauce: 206 Calories; 0.3 g Total Fat; 188 mg Sodium; 2 g Protein; 50 g Carbohydrate; 2 g Dietary Fiber

Pictured on page 126.

Cranberry Hasselback Yams

Pretty to look at and delicious to eat! This dish is a variation of a technique first developed in Stockholm, Sweden.

Brown sugar, packed	½ cup	125 mL
Margarine (or butter), softened	¼ cup	60 mL
Ground cinnamon	⅛ tsp.	0.5 mL
Peeled medium yams	4	4
Dried cranberries (or cherries)	½ cup	125 mL

Combine first 3 ingredients in small bowl. Divide into 4 portions.

Slice yams crosswise ¼ inch (6 mm) thick not quite through so that they are still attached at bottom.

Insert 3 to 4 cranberries in each cut of yam. Spread ¼ of margarine mixture, or about 2 tbsp. (30 mL), on top of each. Wrap each potato tightly in double thickness of foil. Bake in 425°F (220°C) oven for 1 hour. Remove foil, drizzling sauce on each potato. Serves 4.

1 serving: 382 Calories; 12.6 g Total Fat; 164 mg Sodium; 2 g Protein; 67 g Carbohydrate; 7 g Dietary Fiber

Pictured on page 125.

APPLE YAMS: Omit cranberries. Slice 2 cored red apples (such as Spartan or McIntosh) ¼ inch (6 mm) thick. Insert 1 slice in each cut. Bake as above.

HAWAIIAN YAMS: Omit cranberries. Insert about 2 tsp. (10 mL) dried tropical snack (containing dried pineapple cut smaller if necessary, and coconut) in each cut. Bake as above.

Paré Pointer

Bookkeepers are people who never return books they borrow.

Cranberry Sweet Potatoes

Sweetness is tempered by tart cranberries. Try this the next time you serve turkey. Garnish with whole fresh or frozen and thawed cranberries.

Can of sweet potatoes, drained and sliced	19 oz.	540 mL
Whole cranberry sauce	1 cup	250 mL
Prepared orange juice	2 tbsp.	30 mL
Brown sugar, packed	2 tbsp.	30 mL
Margarine (or butter)	1 tbsp.	15 mL
Salt	¼ tsp.	1 mL
Can of sweet potatoes, drained and sliced	19 oz.	540 mL
Finely chopped pecans (optional)	2 tbsp.	30 mL

Layer first amount of sweet potato slices in ungreased 2 quart (2 L) casserole.

Stir next 5 ingredients in small saucepan. Heat and stir until boiling. Spoon ½ of mixture on potato in casserole.

Layer second amount of sweet potato slices on top. Spoon second ½ of cranberry mixture on top.

Sprinkle with pecans. Bake, uncovered, in 350°F (175°C) oven for about 35 minutes until bubbly hot. Serves 6.

1 serving: 249 Calories; 2.3 g Total Fat; 232 mg Sodium; 3 g Protein; 56 g Carbohydrate; 4 g Dietary Fiber

Pictured on page 35.

Candied Sweet Potatoes

Sweet, glossy coating with subtle citrus flavor.

Peeled sweet potatoes, cut into large chunks	1½ lbs.	680 g
Water		
Salt	½ tsp.	2 mL
Prepared orange juice	½ cup	125 mL
Brown sugar, packed	⅓ cup	75 mL
Lemon (or lime) juice	2 tsp.	10 mL
Cornstarch	1 tsp.	5 mL

(continued on next page)

Cook sweet potato in water and salt in large saucepan until barely tender. Do not overcook. Drain. Cool enough to handle. Slice potatoes.

Stir remaining 4 ingredients in frying pan until boiling and slightly thickened. Add potato slices. Cook, stirring gently, on low for 5 to 6 minutes until potatoes are tender and glossy. Serves 6.

1 serving: 179 Calories; 0.4 g Total Fat; 19 mg Sodium; 2 g Protein; 43 g Carbohydrate; 3 g Dietary Fiber

Apricot Sweet Potatoes

Not too sweet, with a crunch from pecans.
Pleasant combination to serve with roast pork or ham.

Baked, peeled sweet potatoes, cut in half lengthwise	2 lbs.	900 g
Can of apricots, drained, syrup reserved	14 oz.	398 mL
Brown sugar, packed	½ cup	125 mL
Cornstarch	1 tbsp.	15 mL
Ground cinnamon	⅛ tsp.	0.5 mL
Lemon juice	1 tsp.	5 mL
Reserved syrup, plus water to make	1 cup	250 mL
Chopped pecans	¼ cup	60 mL

Arrange sweet potato halves, cut side up, in pan large enough to hold in single layer. Arrange apricot halves on top.

Mix brown sugar, cornstarch and cinnamon in small saucepan. Stir in lemon juice and reserved syrup. Heat and stir until boiling and thickened. Pour on sweet potatoes and apricots.

Sprinkle with pecans. Bake, uncovered, in 350°F (175°C) oven for about 30 minutes until hot and bubbly. Serves 6.

1 serving: 201 Calories; 3.6 g Total Fat; 13 mg Sodium; 2 g Protein; 43 g Carbohydrate; 3 g Dietary Fiber

Pictured on front cover.

PEACH SWEET POTATOES: Substitute can of sliced peaches for apricots.

Poutine

Much more economical to make this fast-food favorite at home.

Frozen french fries (shoestring type)	1⅔ lbs.	750 g
Grated part-skim mozzarella cheese	1⅓ cups	325 mL
Water	½ cup	125 mL
All-purpose flour	¼ cup	60 mL
Can of condensed beef broth	10 oz.	284 mL
Pepper	⅛ tsp.	0.5 mL

Spread fries in even layer on large ungreased baking sheet. Bake as directed until crispy. Divide among 4 individual ovenproof bowls or plates.

Sprinkle ⅓ cup (75 mL) cheese over each. Put into hot oven, with heat turned off, until cheese is melted.

Combine water and flour in small saucepan until smooth. Gradually whisk in beef broth. Heat and stir until boiling and thickened. Stir in pepper. Makes 1⅓ cups (325 mL) gravy. Remove bowls from oven. Drizzle ⅓ cup (75 mL) gravy over each serving. Serves 4.

1 serving: 560 Calories; 23.3 g Total Fat; 718 mg Sodium; 19 g Protein; 71 g Carbohydrate; 6 g Dietary Fiber

Creamy Dilled Potatoes

A nice blend of dill and onion. This breaks all the rules but a little cream truly goes a long way.

Peeled waxy potatoes (about 2 medium), cut into chunks	1 lb.	454 g
Water		
Salt	1 tsp.	5 mL
Whipping cream	¼ cup	60 mL
Chopped fresh chives (or tops of green onion)	1½ tbsp.	25 mL
Dill weed	½ tsp.	2 mL

(continued on next page)

Cook potato in water and salt in large saucepan until tender. Drain. Put into medium serving bowl.

Heat whipping cream, chives and dill weed in small saucepan until just boiling. Pour cream mixture over potato. Serves 6.

1 serving: 71 Calories; 3.5 g Total Fat; 6 mg Sodium; 1 g Protein; 9 g Carbohydrate; 1 g Dietary Fiber

Apple Sweet Potato Bake

Serve as an accompaniment to baked ham or pork chops or as dessert with ice cream.

Brown sugar, packed	½ cup	125 mL
Ground cinnamon, just a pinch		
Salt	¼ tsp.	1 mL
Water	¼ cup	60 mL
Peeled, sliced medium cooking apples (such as McIntosh)	4-5	4-5
Baked, peeled, sliced sweet potatoes (see Note)	1½ lbs.	680 g
TOPPING		
Crushed corn flakes cereal	½ cup	125 mL
Margarine (or butter), melted	2 tbsp.	30 mL
Finely chopped pecans	3 tbsp.	50 mL

Combine first 5 ingredients in large saucepan. Simmer, stirring often, until apple slices are softened. Spoon ½ of apple mixture into ungreased 3 quart (3 L) casserole.

Cover with ½ of potato slices. Repeat layers.

Topping: Combine all ingredients in small bowl. Sprinkle on top of casserole. Bake, uncovered, in 350°F (175°C) oven for 20 to 25 minutes until heated through. Serves 6.

1 serving: 318 Calories; 6.5 g Total Fat; 233 mg Sodium; 3 g Protein; 65 g Carbohydrate; 6 g Dietary Fiber

Pictured on page 36.

Note: Substitute two 19 oz. (540 mL) cans drained sweet potatoes for fresh cooked sweet potatoes for a brighter, prettier-looking casserole.

Side Dishes

French-Fried Potatoes

Sometimes you just must have them deep-fried! Try sweet potatoes too.

Peeled or unpeeled medium potatoes (or sweet potatoes), cut into narrow fingers (see Note)	4	4
Cooking oil, for deep-frying		
Salt, sprinkle		

Drop potato strips in small batches into 375°F (190°C) cooking oil. Deep-fry for 9 to 10 minutes until golden brown. Remove with slotted spoon to paper towels to drain.

Sprinkle with salt. Serves 4.

1 serving: 212 Calories; 11.7 g Total Fat; 11 mg Sodium; 3 g Protein; 25 g Carbohydrate; 2 g Dietary Fiber

Note: For better browning, soak potato fingers in cold water for 30 minutes. Dry well.

Broiled Potatoes

Buttery, french-fry taste in these crispy, tender potatoes.

Unpeeled medium potatoes	4	4
Water		
Cooking oil	2 tbsp.	30 mL
Margarine (or butter), melted	2 tbsp.	30 mL
Ground rosemary	¼ tsp.	1 mL
Salt	½ tsp.	2 mL
Pepper	⅛ tsp.	0.5 mL

Cook whole potatoes in water in large saucepan for about 30 minutes until tender. Cool enough to handle. Peel. Cut into ¼ inch (6 mm) slices. Arrange in single layer on greased baking sheet.

Stir next 5 ingredients well in cup. Using pastry brush, dab each slice with mixture. Broil for about 15 minutes until golden and crispy. Turn slices over. Dab each slice with mixture. Broil for about 10 minutes until golden and crispy. Serves 4.

1 serving: 225 Calories; 12.4 g Total Fat; 409 mg Sodium; 2 g Protein; 27 g Carbohydrate; 2 g Dietary Fiber

Grilled Potato Packets

Everyone gets their own seasoned portion.

Peeled, sliced medium potatoes	6	6
Margarine (or butter)	¼ cup	60 mL
Onion salt	½ tsp.	2 mL
Garlic salt	¼ tsp.	1 mL
Celery salt	¼ tsp.	1 mL
Onion powder	¼ tsp.	1 mL
Paprika	½ tsp.	2 mL
Freshly ground pepper, sprinkle		
Grated Parmesan cheese	¼ cup	60 mL

Using double thickness of 10 inch (25 cm) square foil for each potato, overlap 2 or 3 rows of potato slices on each.

Melt margarine in cup in microwave. Stir in next 5 ingredients. Drizzle about 2 tsp. (10 mL) over each potato.

Sprinkle with pepper and cheese. Seal foil. Grill over medium heat for 15 minutes. Turn. Grill for 15 to 20 minutes until tender. Serves 6.

1 serving: 184 Calories; 9.7 g Total Fat; 412 mg Sodium; 4 g Protein; 21 g Carbohydrate; 2 g Dietary Fiber

Variation: These can also be cooked in 350°F (175°C) oven for about 35 minutes.

 *For fluffier mashed potatoes, use skim milk powder instead of regular milk.*

Super Creamed Potatoes

Saucy potatoes, perfect to serve with baked pork chops or chicken.

Peeled, diced potatoes	6 cups	1.5 L
Chopped onion	1 cup	250 mL
Water		
Salt	½ tsp.	2 mL
Milk	⅔ cup	150 mL
Grated light sharp Cheddar cheese	1 cup	250 mL
Salt	½ tsp.	2 mL
Pepper	⅛ tsp.	0.5 mL
Chopped fresh parsley	2 tbsp.	30 mL
Grated Parmesan cheese (optional)	2 tbsp.	30 mL

Cook potato and onion in water and first amount of salt in medium saucepan until potato is tender. Drain well.

Add milk, Cheddar cheese, salt, pepper and parsley. Heat, stirring often, until cheese is melted.

Sprinkle with Parmesan cheese. Serves 6.

1 serving: 142 Calories; 4.4 g Total Fat; 373 mg Sodium; 7 g Protein; 18 g Carbohydrate; 1 g Dietary Fiber

Sour Potatoes

Good tart flavor in these very saucy potatoes. Eastern European roots.

Peeled, cubed potatoes	6 cups	1.5 L
Chopped onion	1 cup	250 mL
Small bay leaf	1	1
Salt	1 tsp.	5 mL
Pepper	¼ tsp.	1 mL
Water	1½ cups	375 mL
Light sour cream	1 cup	250 mL
White vinegar	1 tbsp.	15 mL
Granulated sugar	1 tbsp.	15 mL
Chopped chives	1 tbsp.	15 mL

(continued on next page)

Cook potato, onion, bay leaf, salt and pepper in water in medium saucepan until potatoes are tender. Do not drain. Discard bay leaf.

Mix sour cream, vinegar, sugar and chives in small bowl. Stir into potato. Bring to a boil. Let stand for 15 minutes for sauce to thicken. Serves 6.

1 serving: 115 Calories; 3 g Total Fat; 475 mg Sodium; 3 g Protein; 20 g Carbohydrate; 2 g Dietary Fiber

Creamed Potatoes

Hint of nutmeg adds a pleasant aftertaste. A European dish.

Peeled, quartered potatoes (about 6 medium)	2 lbs.	900 g
Water		
Salt	½ tsp.	2 mL
Margarine (or butter)	2 tbsp.	30 mL
All-purpose flour	2 tbsp.	30 mL
Milk	1 cup	250 mL
Salt	½ tsp.	2 mL
Pepper	¼ tsp.	1 mL
Ground nutmeg	⅛ tsp.	0.5 mL
Chopped fresh parsley	2 tbsp.	30 mL

Cook potato in water and first amount of salt in medium saucepan until tender. Drain. Cool enough to handle. Cut into cubes or slices. Return to saucepan.

Melt margarine in small saucepan. Mix in flour until smooth. Stir in next 5 ingredients until boiling and thickened. Pour over potato. Heat, stirring gently, until hot. Serves 6.

1 serving: 141 Calories; 4.5 g Total Fat; 299 mg Sodium; 3 g Protein; 22 g Carbohydrate; 1 g Dietary Fiber

Variation: Add crisp and crumbled cooked bacon (as much as you like) and 1 tbsp. (15 mL) fresh chopped dill for a lovely change.

Champ

Little potato volcanoes filled with butter. An Irish treat.

Peeled potatoes (about 4 medium), cut up	2 lbs.	900 g
Water		
Milk	¾ cup	175 mL
Green onions, chopped	10	10
Salt	1 tsp.	5 ml
Pepper	¼ tsp.	1 mL
Butter	6 tbsp.	100 mL

Cook potato in boiling water in large saucepan until tender. Drain. Mash.

Bring milk to a boil in medium saucepan. Add onion, salt and pepper. Simmer for 5 minutes.

Add potato. Mash well. Shape into 6 mounds on individual serving plates. Make small well in center of each mound. Add 1 tbsp. (15 mL) butter in pieces to each well. Serves 6.

1 serving: 250 Calories; 12.2 g Total Fat; 596 mg Sodium; 4 g Protein; 33 g Carbohydrate; 2 g Dietary Fiber

Variation: This may be made into 1 large mound with all butter in center well, but it is better that everyone has his/her own well of butter.

Potato Re-Run

When you have leftover baked potatoes, these are a snap to make!

Margarine (or butter)	1 tbsp.	15 mL
Peeled, cooked, cubed (or diced) potatoes	3 cups	750 mL
Parsley flakes (or chopped chives)	1 tsp.	5 mL
Salt	¼ tsp.	1 mL
Pepper, sprinkle		

Melt margarine in non-stick frying pan until sizzling. Add potato, parsley, salt and pepper. Cover. Heat, stirring often, until browned. See Tip, below. Serves 4.

1 serving: 128 Calories; 3.1 g Total Fat; 210 mg Sodium; 2 g Protein; 24 g Carbohydrate; 2 g Dietary Fiber

Chocolates

Sweet fondant can be flavored and colored for variety as you like.

Mashed potatoes	½ cup	125 mL
Cooking oil	1 tsp.	5 mL
Salt, just a pinch		
Icing (confectioner's) sugar	3 cups	750 mL
Flavoring, to taste (see Note)		
Food coloring (optional), see Note		
COATING		
Semisweet chocolate chips	1 cup	250 mL
Grated paraffin wax	3 tbsp.	50 mL

Mix first 4 ingredients well in medium bowl. Knead to incorporate icing sugar. Divide into portions if making more than 1 flavor.

Mix in flavoring starting with ⅛ to ¼ tsp. (0.5 to 1 mL). Add a drop of liquid or paste food color and knead until even in color. If mixture becomes sticky, knead in 1 tbsp. (15 mL) of icing sugar. Shape into ½ inch (12 mm) balls.

Coating: Melt chocolate chips and grated paraffin in small saucepan on low, stirring often, until smooth. Coat balls. Lift out of chocolate with fork, draining into pan. Let stand on waxed paper until firm. Makes about 100 chocolates.

1 chocolate: 23 Calories; 0.6 g Total Fat; trace Sodium; trace Protein; 5 g Carbohydrate; trace Dietary Fiber

Note: Artificial and pure extracts such as vanilla, orange, peppermint, maple, strawberry and cherry may be used. Finely grated fresh orange and lemon zest can be used as well. Coordinate colors to go with flavor. For example, pink for strawberry and cherry flavors, green for peppermint and spearmint flavors.

Variation: Substitute chocolate dipping wafers for chocolate chips and grated paraffin wax.

Paré Pointer

Flowers are so lazy. They're always in beds.

Chocolate Cake

A moist, tender cake you will be proud to serve.

Margarine (or butter), softened	½ cup	125 mL
Granulated sugar	1 cup	250 mL
Large eggs	2	2
Vanilla	1 tsp.	5 mL
Buttermilk (or reconstituted from powder)	1 cup	250 mL
Mashed potatoes	1 cup	250 mL
All-purpose flour	1¾ cups	425 mL
Cocoa, sifted	⅓ cup	75 mL
Baking powder	1 tsp.	5 mL
Baking soda	½ tsp.	2 mL
Ground cinnamon	½ tsp.	2 mL
Salt	½ tsp.	2 mL

Chocolate Icing (see page 141)

Cream margarine and sugar in large bowl. Beat in eggs, 1 at a time. Add vanilla. Mix.

Slowly beat buttermilk into potato in small bowl until smooth. Beat into egg mixture.

Stir next 6 ingredients in medium bowl. Add to potato mixture. Beat slowly to incorporate flour. Beat on medium for about 1 minute until smooth. Turn into greased 9 x 9 inch (22 x 22 cm) pan. Bake, uncovered, in 350°F (175°C) oven for about 40 minutes until wooden pick inserted in center comes out clean. Cool.

Ice with Chocolate Icing. Cuts into 16 pieces.

1 piece: 185 Calories; 4.8 g Total Fat; 151 mg Sodium; 3 g Protein; 34 g Carbohydrate; 1 g Dietary Fiber

Pictured on page 144.

ORANGE CHOCOLATE CAKE: Omit cinnamon. Add 2 tsp. (10 mL) finely grated orange peel to wet ingredients.

CHIP CHOCOLATE CAKE: Stir in ½ cup (125 mL) mini semisweet chocolate chips to batter before turning into pan.

Chocolate Icing

No dairy products or fat in this icing.

Warm mashed potatoes	¼ cup	60 mL
Icing (confectioner's) sugar	2¾ cups	675 mL
Cocoa, sifted	2 tbsp.	30 mL
Vanilla	½ tsp.	2 mL
Warm water (or coffee), approximately	2 tbsp.	30 mL

Sieve or rice potatoes into medium bowl.

Sift icing sugar and cocoa into potatoes. Stir.

Slowly beat in vanilla and water, adding more water or icing sugar to make desired spreading consistency. Makes 1¼ cups (300 mL).

1 tbsp. (15 mL): 66 Calories; 0.1 g Total Fat; trace Sodium; trace Protein; 17 g Carbohydrate; trace Dietary Fiber

Pictured on page 144.

Pinwheels

So pretty and such a sweet treat!

Mashed potatoes	⅓ cup	75 mL
Vanilla	½ tsp.	2 mL
Icing (confectioner's) sugar, approximately	2½ cups	625 mL
Salt	⅛ tsp.	0.5 mL
Peanut butter	⅓ cup	75 mL

Stir potato, vanilla and icing sugar in large bowl. Turn out onto surface dusted with icing sugar. Knead until smooth, adding a bit more icing sugar if necessary to make pliable but non-sticky dough. Divide into 3 equal portions. Roll each portion ⅛ inch (3 mm) thick into 5 x 8 inch (12.5 x 20 cm) rectangle on surface dusted with icing sugar.

Spread with ⅓ of peanut butter (about 1½ tbsp., 25 mL). Roll up from long side like jelly roll. Wrap with plastic wrap. Chill. Cut into ¼ inch (6 mm) slices. Makes about 5½ to 6 dozen pinwheels.

1 pinwheel: 27 Calories; 0.7 g Total Fat; 12 mg Sodium; trace Protein; 5 g Carbohydrate; trace Dietary Fiber

Pictured on page 144.

Mince Pie

Serve à la mode while still warm.

Brown sugar, packed	½ cup	125 mL
All-purpose flour	¼ cup	60 mL
Ground cinnamon	½ tsp.	2 mL
Ground nutmeg	¼ tsp.	1 mL
Ground cloves	¼ tsp.	1 mL
Salt	¼ tsp.	1 mL
White vinegar	2 tbsp.	30 mL
Water	½ cup	125 mL
Peeled, finely grated potato	1 cup	250 mL
Peeled, chopped apple	1 cup	250 mL
Unbaked 9 inch (22 cm) pie shells	2	2
Granulated sugar	¼-½ tsp.	1-2 mL

Stir first 6 ingredients in large bowl.

Add vinegar, water, potato and apple. Stir well.

Spoon filling into one pie shell. Dampen outside edge and top with second flattened crust. Trim and crimp edges. Cut slits in top.

Sprinkle with granulated sugar. Bake on bottom rack in 350°F (175°C) oven for 60 minutes. Cover top with foil if pie becomes too dark. Cuts into 8 wedges.

1 wedge: 312 Calories; 15.2 g Total Fat; 366 mg Sodium; 3 g Protein; 41 g Carbohydrate; 1 g Dietary Fiber

1. Potato Wheat Biscuits, page 19
2. Sesame Sticks, page 14
3. Asparagus Chowder, page 33

Props Courtesy Of: Chintz & Company
The Bay

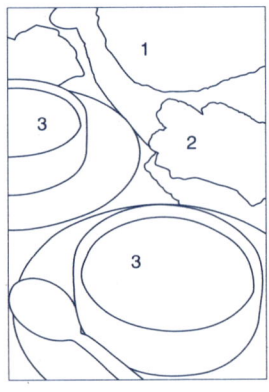

Drop Cookies

Comforting, soft cookies with a hint of sweet cherries.

Hard margarine (or butter), softened	½ cup	125 mL
Brown sugar, packed	1 cup	250 mL
Large egg, fork-beaten	1	1
Orange flavoring	½ tsp.	2 mL
Lemon flavoring	½ tsp.	2 mL
Mashed potatoes	1 cup	250 mL
Chopped maraschino cherries, blotted dry	½ cup	125 mL
Chopped walnuts	½ cup	125 mL
All-purpose flour	1½ cups	375 mL
Baking powder	1 tsp.	5 mL
Baking soda	½ tsp.	2 mL
Salt	¼ tsp.	1 mL

Cream margarine and sugar in medium bowl. Beat in egg. Add both flavorings and potato. Mix well. Stir in cherries and walnuts.

Stir flour, baking powder, baking soda and salt in small bowl. Add to batter. Stir to moisten. Drop by tablespoonfuls (15 mL) onto greased baking sheet. Bake in 350°F (175°C) oven for 15 to 20 minutes. Makes 3½ dozen cookies.

1 cookie: 78 Calories; 3.5 g Total Fat; 64 mg Sodium; 1 g Protein; 11 g Carbohydrate; trace Dietary Fiber

Pictured on page 144.

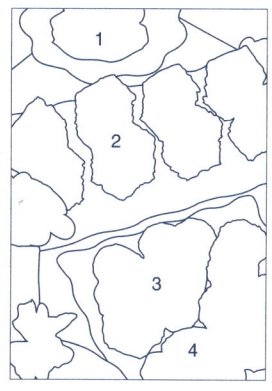

1. Pinwheels, page 141
2. Chocolate Cake, page 140, with Chocolate Icing, page 141
3. Chocolate Cookies, page 146
4. Drop Cookies, above

Props Courtesy Of: Le Gnome

Chocolate Cookies

A cakey-type soft cookie with rich chocolate flavor.

Hard margarine (or butter), softened	½ cup	125 mL
Granulated sugar	½ cup	125 mL
Brown sugar, packed	½ cup	125 mL
Large egg	1	1
Mashed potatoes	½ cup	125 mL
Vanilla	½ tsp.	2 mL
Buttermilk (or reconstituted from powder)	¾ cup	175 mL
All-purpose flour	2 cups	500 mL
Cocoa	⅓ cup	75 mL
Baking soda	½ tsp.	2 mL
Salt	½ tsp.	2 mL

Cream margarine and both sugars in large bowl. Mix in egg, potato, vanilla and buttermilk.

Add remaining 4 ingredients. Stir to moisten. Drop dough by rounded tablespoonfuls (15 mL) onto greased baking sheet. Bake in 400°F (205°C) oven for 10 minutes. Makes 4 dozen cookies.

1 cookie: 62 Calories; 2.3 g Total Fat; 73 mg Sodium; 1 g Protein; 10 g Carbohydrate; 1 g Dietary Fiber

Pictured on page 144.

Candy Squares

Coconut macaroon base with a thick chocolate top.
Reminds you of a certain chocolate bar!

Mashed potatoes	½ cup	125 mL
Hard margarine (or butter), softened	1 tbsp.	15 mL
Vanilla	1 tsp.	5 mL
Salt	¼ tsp.	1 mL
Icing (confectioner's) sugar	3 cups	750 mL
Medium unsweetened coconut	2½ cups	625 mL
Semisweet chocolate chips	1 cup	250 mL
Hard margarine (or butter)	2 tbsp.	30 mL

(continued on next page)

Stir potato, first amount of margarine, vanilla and salt in large bowl.

Mix in icing sugar and coconut. Press firmly in greased 8 x 8 inch (20 x 20 cm) pan.

Melt chocolate chips and second amount of margarine in medium saucepan on low, stirring often. Spread on top of squares. Chill for 1 hour. Cuts into 50 squares.

1 square: 83 Calories; 4.8 g Total Fat; 24 mg Sodium; 1 g Protein; 11 g Carbohydrate; trace Dietary Fiber

Sweet Potato Pie

A nice replacement for traditional pumpkin pie.

Large eggs	3	3
Can of sweet potatoes, drained and mashed	19 oz.	540 mL
Granulated sugar	¼ cup	60 mL
Corn syrup	2 tbsp.	30 mL
Ground nutmeg	¼ tsp.	1 mL
Ground cinnamon	¼ tsp.	1 mL
All-purpose flour	2 tbsp.	30 mL
Salt	¼ tsp.	1 mL
Milk	½ cup	125 mL
Unbaked 9 inch (22 cm) pie shell	1	1
Frozen whipped topping, thawed	2 cups	500 mL

Beat eggs in large bowl until light. Add sweet potato, sugar, corn syrup, nutmeg, cinnamon, flour and salt. Beat well.

Slowly beat in milk.

Pour into prepared pie shell. Bake on bottom rack in 400°F (205°C) oven for 10 minutes. Reduce heat to 350°F (175°C). Bake for about 40 minutes until knife inserted near center comes out clean. Cool, then chill.

Cover with whipped topping. Cuts into 8 wedges.

1 wedge: 311 Calories; 14.7 g Total Fat; 293 mg Sodium; 6 g Protein; 40 g Carbohydrate; 2 g Dietary Fiber

Sweet Potato Cheesecake

Reminiscent of pumpkin pie. Not as rich as most cheesecakes.

CRUST		
Hard margarine (or butter)	¼ cup	60 mL
Gingersnap cookie crumbs	1¼ cups	300 mL
FILLING		
Light cream cheese, softened	8 oz.	250 g
Granulated sugar	½ cup	125 mL
Light creamed cottage cheese, smoothed in blender	1 cup	250 mL
Can of sweet potatoes, drained and mashed	19 oz.	540 mL
All-purpose flour	2 tbsp.	30 mL
Ground cinnamon	¾ tsp.	4 mL
Ground nutmeg	½ tsp.	2 mL
Ground ginger	½ tsp.	2 mL
Large eggs	2	2

Crust: Melt margarine in medium saucepan. Stir in crumbs. Press firmly on bottom of ungreased 9 inch (22 cm) springform pan. Bake in 350°F (175°C) oven for 10 minutes.

Filling: Beat cream cheese, sugar and cottage cheese until smooth. Mix in sweet potato, flour, cinnamon, nutmeg and ginger.

Add eggs, 1 at a time, beating on low just to mix in. Turn into crust. Bake in 350°F (175°C) oven for about 60 minutes until firm. Run a knife around top edge of cheesecake so it will settle evenly. Cool, then chill. Cuts into 12 wedges.

1 wedge: 245 Calories; 10.1 g Total Fat; 447 mg Sodium; 7 g Protein; 32 g Carbohydrate; 1 g Dietary Fiber

To prevent scalloped potatoes from curdling, bring sliced potatoes in water in a saucepan just to a boil. Drain immediately and use as recipe states.

Sweet Potato Dessert

Very sweet. Delicious served with unsweetened whipped cream.

Mashed sweet potatoes	4 cups	1 L
Granulated sugar	1 tbsp.	15 mL
Large egg, fork-beaten	1	1
Vanilla	½ tsp.	2 mL
Salt	½ tsp.	2 mL
Small banana, mashed	1	1
Prepared orange juice	¼ cup	60 mL
Brown sugar, packed	2 tbsp.	30 mL
TOPPING		
Hard margarine (or butter)	¼ cup	60 mL
Brown sugar, packed	½ cup	125 mL
All-purpose flour	¼ cup	60 mL
Chopped pecans	½ cup	125 mL

Mix first 5 ingredients in medium bowl. Turn into greased 2 quart (2 L) casserole.

Mix banana, orange juice and brown sugar in small bowl. Spread on sweet potato mixture.

Topping: Melt margarine in small saucepan. Stir in brown sugar, flour and pecans. Sprinkle on casserole. Bake in 350°F (175°C) oven for 30 minutes. Serves 8.

1 serving: 400 Calories; 12.6 g Total Fat; 278 mg Sodium; 5 g Protein; 69 g Carbohydrate; 5 g Dietary Fiber

Paré Pointer

Adam's first day was awfully long because there wasn't any Eve.

Steamed Pudding

Grated potato provides the moistness and texture, replacing beef suet in a traditional pudding! Try it with a small scoop of ice cream or your favorite hard sauce.

Hard margarine (or butter), softened	½ cup	125 mL
Brown sugar, packed	¾ cup	175 mL
Fancy (mild) molasses	¼ cup	60 mL
Peeled, grated potatoes	2 cups	500 mL
Raisins	1 cup	250 mL
Cut mixed glazed fruit	1 cup	250 mL
All-purpose flour	1½ cups	375 mL
Baking soda	1 tsp.	5 mL
Salt	½ tsp.	2 mL
Ground cinnamon	1 tsp.	5 mL
Ground nutmeg	½ tsp.	2 mL
Ground allspice	½ tsp.	2 mL

Cream margarine, sugar and molasses in large bowl. Stir in potato, raisins and fruit.

Mix remaining 6 ingredients well in medium bowl. Add to pudding. Mix well. Turn into greased 6 cup (1.5 L) pudding pan or deep round glass bowl. Cover with foil, tying down sides securely with string. Set into steamer with boiling water halfway up sides of pudding pan or bowl. Cover. Simmer for 3 hours, adding more boiling water as needed. Serves 12.

1 serving: 321 Calories; 8.5 g Total Fat; 343 mg Sodium; 3 g Protein; 61 g Carbohydrate; 2 g Dietary Fiber

When time is short and you want baked potatoes, boil them for about 10 minutes before baking in oven at 400°F (205°C) for 30 minutes.

Measurement Tables

Throughout this book measurements are given in Conventional and Metric measure. To compensate for differences between the two measurements due to rounding, a full metric measure is not always used. The cup used is the standard 8 fluid ounce. Temperature is given in degrees Fahrenheit and Celsius. Baking pan measurements are in inches and centimetres as well as quarts and litres. An exact metric conversion is given below as well as the working equivalent (Standard Measure).

Spoons

Conventional Measure	Metric Exact Conversion Millilitre (mL)	Metric Standard Measure Millilitre (mL)
1/8 teaspoon (tsp.)	0.6 mL	0.5 mL
1/4 teaspoon (tsp.)	1.2 mL	1 mL
1/2 teaspoon (tsp.)	2.4 mL	2 mL
1 teaspoon (tsp.)	4.7 mL	5 mL
2 teaspoons (tsp.)	9.4 mL	10 mL
1 tablespoon (tbsp.)	14.2 mL	15 mL

Cups

Conventional Measure	Metric Exact Conversion Millilitre (mL)	Metric Standard Measure Millilitre (mL)
1/4 cup (4 tbsp.)	56.8 mL	60 mL
1/3 cup (5 1/3 tbsp.)	75.6 mL	75 mL
1/2 cup (8 tbsp.)	113.7 mL	125 mL
2/3 cup (10 2/3 tbsp.)	151.2 mL	150 mL
3/4 cup (12 tbsp.)	170.5 mL	175 mL
1 cup (16 tbsp.)	227.3 mL	250 mL
4 1/2 cups	1022.9 mL	1000 mL (1 L)

Oven Temperatures

Fahrenheit (°F)	Celsius (°C)
175°	80°
200°	95°
225°	110°
250°	120°
275°	140°
300°	150°
325°	160°
350°	175°
375°	190°
400°	205°
425°	220°
450°	230°
475°	240°
500°	260°

Dry Measurements

Conventional Measure Ounces (oz.)	Metric Exact Conversion Grams (g)	Metric Standard Measure Grams (g)
1 oz.	28.3 g	28 g
2 oz.	56.7 g	57 g
3 oz.	85.0 g	85 g
4 oz.	113.4 g	125 g
5 oz.	141.7 g	140 g
6 oz.	170.1 g	170 g
7 oz.	198.4 g	200 g
8 oz.	226.8 g	250 g
16 oz.	453.6 g	500 g
32 oz.	907.2 g	1000 g (1 kg)

Pans

Conventional Inches	Metric Centimetres
8x8 inch	20x20 cm
9x9 inch	22x22 cm
9x13 inch	22x33 cm
10x15 inch	25x38 cm
11x17 inch	28x43 cm
8x2 inch round	20x5 cm
9x2 inch round	22x5 cm
10x4 1/2 inch tube	25x11 cm
8x4x3 inch loaf	20x10x7.5 cm
9x5x3 inch loaf	22x12.5x7.5 cm

Casseroles

CANADA & BRITAIN Standard Size Casserole	Exact Metric Measure	UNITED STATES Standard Size Casserole	Exact Metric Measure
1 qt. (5 cups)	1.13 L	1 qt. (5 cups)	900 mL
1 1/2 qts. (7 1/2 cups)	1.69 L	1 1/2 qts. (7 1/2 cups)	1.35 L
2 qts. (10 cups)	2.25 L	2 qts. (10 cups)	1.8 L
2 1/2 qts. (12 1/2 cups)	2.81 L	2 1/2 qts. (12 1/2 cups)	2.25 L
3 qts. (15 cups)	3.38 L	3 qts. (15 cups)	2.7 L
4 qts. (20 cups)	4.5 L	4 qts. (20 cups)	3.6 L
5 qts. (25 cups)	5.63 L	5 qts. (25 cups)	4.5 L

Index

A

All-In-One Breakfast 78
Appetizers
   Cheesy Potato Skins 16
   Dilly Potato Tots 14
   Gnocchi With Sauce 43
   Potato Appetizer Puffs 13
   Samosas 15
   Sesame Sticks 14
   Sweet Potato Balls 12
   Tourtière Turnovers 51
   Vegetable Squares 12
   Veggie Fritters 11
Apple Sweet Potato Bake 133
Apple Yams 129
Apricot Sweet Potatoes 131
Asparagus Chowder 33

B

Bacon And Cheese Spuds 124
Baked
   Bacon And Cheese Spuds . . . 124
   Broccoli-Stuffed Potatoes . . . 121
   Cheese-Stuffed Potatoes 120
   Full O' Beans Spud 120
   Kids' Stuffed Spuds 123
   Reuben-Stuffed Potatoes . . . 122
   Sour Cream-Stuffed Potatoes 122
Baked Fries 118
Baked Potato Salad 38
Bean Potato Bake 55
Bean Potato Cake 95
Biscuits
   Potato 20
   Potato Wheat 19
   Quickest Potato 20
Boxty 83
Breads & Buns
   Brown Grain Bread 24
   Cheddar Hotcakes 23
   Cinnamon Buns 22
   Cinnamon Doughnuts 28
   Currant Scones 21
   Deluxe Cheese And Onion
      Hotcakes 23
   Doughnuts 28
   Green Onion Hotcakes 23
   Potato Biscuits 20
   Potato Bread 26
   Potato Buns 27
   Potato Hotcakes 23
   Potato Tray Buns 27
   Potato Wheat Biscuits 19
   Quickest Potato Biscuits 20
   Sugared Doughnuts 28
   Sweet Potato Loaf 25
Breakfast
   All-In-One 78
   Cheddar Hotcakes 23
   Deluxe Cheese And Onion
      Hotcakes 23
   Green Onion Hotcakes 23
   Potato Cheese Frittata 74
   Potato Frittata 74
   Potato Hotcakes 23
   Potato Quiche 76
   Sausage Frittata 75

Spanish Omelet 76
Broccoli-Stuffed Potatoes 121
Broiled Potatoes 134
Brown Grain Bread 24
Browned Onion With Potatoes 106
Buns, see Breads & Buns

C

Cakes, Savory
   Bean Potato 95
   Chili Potato 95
   Fish 60
   Meaty Potato 95
   Potato 94
Cakes, Sweet
   Chip Chocolate 140
   Chocolate 140
   Orange Chocolate 140
Candied Sweet Potatoes 130
Candy Squares 146
Casseroles
   Apple Sweet Potato Bake . . . 133
   Bean Potato Bake 55
   Chantilly Potatoes 111
   Cheesy Potatoes And Wieners 52
   Chicken Pot Pie 47
   Coconut Potatoes 80
   Company Potatoes 97
   Con Queso Potatoes 102
   Cranberry Sweet Potatoes . . 130
   Creamy Spinach Potatoes . . . 113
   Deluxe Potatoes 109
   Duchess Potato 87
   Dumpling 48
   Garlic Company Potatoes . . . 97
   Gratin Dauphinois 68
   Gratin Hash Browns 101
   Jalapeño Potatoes 65
   Mashed Ricotta Potatoes . . . 104
   Moussaka 50
   Oven Potatoes Lyonnaise 67
   Parmesan Hash Browns . . . 103
   Potato Mushroom Bake 66
   Potato Puff 112
   Potato Soufflé 77
   Potatoes Anna 100
   Potatoes Parmesan 70
   Potatoes With Mushrooms . . 114
   Quick Scallop Bake 73
   Scalloped Potatoes 69
   Seafood Delight 58
   Shepherd's Pie 49
   Shrimp Pot Pie 59
   Sweet Potato Bake 127
   Sweet Potato Dessert 149
   Tater-Topped Beef Bake 45
   Tomato Potato 66
Celery Cream Soup 31
Champ 138
Chantilly Potatoes 111
Cheddar Hotcakes 23
Cheese Fries 117
Cheese-Stuffed Potatoes 120
Cheesy Potato Skins 16
Cheesy Potatoes And Wieners . 52
Chicken Pot Pie 47
Chili Fries 117
Chili Potato Cake 95
Chip Chocolate Cake 140

Chocolate Cake 140
Chocolate Cookies 146
Chocolate Icing 141
Chocolates 139
Cinnamon Buns 22
Cinnamon Doughnuts 28
Coconut Potatoes 80
Colcannon 110
Company Potatoes 97
Con Queso Potatoes 102
Cookies
   Chocolate 146
   Drop 145
   Pinwheels 141
Cranberry Hasselback Yams . . . 129
Cranberry Sweet Potatoes . . . 130
Cream Sauce 62
Creamed Potatoes 137
Creamed Veggies 62
Creamy Dilled Potatoes 132
Creamy Meat Shells 99
Creamy Potatoes 111
Creamy Spinach Potatoes 113
Cullen Skink 32
Currant Scones 21

D

Deluxe Cheese And Onion
   Hotcakes 23
Deluxe Potatoes 109
Desserts
   Apple Sweet Potato Bake . . . 133
   Candy Squares 146
   Chip Chocolate Cake 140
   Chocolate Cake 140
   Chocolate Cookies 146
   Chocolate Icing 141
   Chocolates 139
   Cinnamon Doughnuts 28
   Doughnuts 28
   Drop Cookies 145
   Mince Pie 142
   Orange Chocolate Cake 140
   Pinwheels 141
   Steamed Pudding 150
   Sugared Doughnuts 28
   Sweet Potato 149
   Sweet Potato Cheesecake . . . 148
   Sweet Potato Pie 147
Dilly Potato Salad 41
Dilly Potato Tots 14
Double Cheese Potatoes 115
Doughnuts 28
Drop Cookies 145
Duchess Cheese Potatoes 87
Duchess Potato Casserole 87
Duchess Potatoes 87
Dumpling Casserole 48

E

Extra Cheesy Potatoes 115

F

Fish Cakes 60
French-Fried Potatoes 134
Fries
   Baked 118

152

Broiled Potatoes 134
Cheese 117
Chili 117
French-Fried Potatoes 134
Oven 117
Poutine 132
Full O' Beans Spud 120

G
Garlic Company Potatoes 97
Garlic Mashed Potatoes 110
German Potato Salad 39
Glazed Garlic Potatoes 62
Gnocchi With Sauce 43
Gold Roast Potatoes 117
Grated Potato Rösti 82
Gratin Dauphinois 68
Gratin Hash Browns 101
Green Onion Hotcakes 23
Grilled Potato Packets 135

H
Hash Brown Pizza Crust 56
Hash Browns
   Con Queso Potatoes 102
   Gratin 101
   Parmesan 103
   Pizza 56
   Potato Heaps 102
   Potato Quiche 76
   Spudonion Pizza 57
   Vegetable Squares 12
Hasselback Potatoes 68
Hawaiian Yams 129
Heaven And Earth 112
Horseradish Potatoes 114
Hotcakes
   Cheddar 23
   Deluxe Cheese And Onion . . . 23
   Green Onion 23
   Potato 23

I
Instant Potatoes
   Gnocchi With Sauce 43
   Speedy Potato Patties 105
International
   Boxty 83
   Coconut Potatoes 80
   Con Queso Potatoes 102
   Cranberry Hasselback Yams . 129
   Creamed Potatoes 137
   Cullen Skink 32
   Duchess Cheese Potatoes . . . 87
   Duchess Potato Casserole . . . 87
   Duchess Potatoes 87
   German Potato Salad 39
   Grated Potato Rösti 82
   Gratin Dauphinois 68
   Hasselback Potatoes 68
   Hawaiian Yams 129
   Heaven And Earth 112
   Jalapeño Potatoes 65
   Latkes 82
   Meaty Roulade 44
   Mixed Duchess Potatoes 87
   Moussaka 50

Noisettes 91
Oven Potatoes Lyonnaise 67
Parmesan Duchess Potatoes . 87
Perogies 84
Potato Cheese Frittata 74
Potato Croquettes 92
Potato Dumplings 79
Potato Frittata 74
Potato Lyonnaise 88
Potato Stir-Fry 81
Potatoes Anna 100
Potatoes Bolognese 46
Potatoes Dauphine 86
Potatoes Dauphine Parmesan . 86
Potatoes O'Brien 80
Poutine 132
Samosas 15
Sausage Frittata 75
Sour Potatoes 136
Tourtière Turnovers 51
Vichyssoise 30
Italian Potato Roast 119

J
Jalapeño Potatoes 65

K
Kids' Stuffed Spuds 123

L
Latkes 82
Layered Potato Salad 40

M
Main Dishes
   Bean Potato Bake 55
   Cheesy Potatoes And Wieners . 52
   Chicken Pot Pie 47
   Dumpling Casserole 48
   Fish Cakes 60
   Gnocchi With Sauce 43
   Meaty Roulade 44
   Moussaka 50
   Pizza Hash Brown 56
   Potatoes Bolognese 46
   Seafood Delight 58
   Shepherd's Pie 49
   Shrimp Pot Pie 59
   Spudonion Pizza 57
   Tater-Topped Beef Bake 45
   Tourtière Turnovers 51
Mashed
   Bean Potato Cake 95
   Boxty 83
   Brown Grain Bread 24
   Browned Onion With
      Potatoes 106
   Candy Squares 146
   Celery Cream Soup 31
   Champ 138
   Chantilly Potatoes 111
   Cheddar Hotcakes 23
   Chili Potato Cake 95
   Chip Chocolate Cake 140
   Chocolate Cake 140

Chocolate Cookies 146
Chocolate Icing 141
Chocolates 139
Cinnamon Buns 22
Cinnamon Doughnuts 28
Colcannon 110
Company Potatoes 97
Creamy Meat Shells 99
Creamy Potatoes 111
Creamy Spinach Potatoes . . . 113
Cullen Skink 32
Currant Scones 21
Deluxe Cheese And Onion
   Hotcakes 23
Deluxe Potatoes 109
Double Cheese Potatoes . . . 115
Doughnuts 28
Drop Cookies 145
Duchess Cheese Potatoes 87
Duchess Potato Casserole . . . 87
Duchess Potatoes 87
Dumpling Cassserole 48
Extra Cheesy Potatoes 115
Fish Cakes 60
Garlic Company Potatoes 97
Garlic Mashed Potatoes 110
Green Onion Hotcakes 23
Heaven And Earth 112
Horseradish Potatoes 114
Meaty Potato Cake 95
Meaty Roulade 44
Mixed Duchess Potatoes 87
Mushroom Cheese Braids . . . 96
Orange Chocolate Cake 140
Parmesan Duchess Potatoes . 87
Perogies 84
Pinwheels 141
Potato And Cheese Filling . . . 84
Potato And Onion Filling 84
Potato Appetizer Puffs 13
Potato Biscuits 20
Potato Bread 26
Potato Buns 27
Potato Cake 94
Potato Crunchies 118
Potato Dumplings 79
Potato Hotcakes 23
Potato Parcels 95
Potato Puff Balls 100
Potato Puff Casserole 112
Potato Sausage Soup 32
Potato Soufflé 77
Potato Stuffing 61
Potato Tray Buns 27
Potato Wheat Biscuits 19
Potatoes Dauphine 86
Potatoes Dauphine Parmesan . 86
Potatoes With Mushrooms . . 114
Quick Cheese Potatoes 119
Quickest Potato Biscuits 20
Samosas 15
Seafood Delight 58
Sesame Sticks 14
Speedy Cheesy Potatoes . . . 104
Sugared Doughnuts 28
Sweet Potato Bake 127
Sweet Potato Cheesecake . . . 148
Sweet Potato Dessert 149
Sweet Potato Dumplings 48

153

Sweet Potato Loaf 25
Sweet Potato Pie 147
Vegetables In Shells 98
Mashed Potato Soup. 34
Mashed Ricotta Potatoes 104
Meaty Potato Cake 95
Meaty Roulade 44
Mince Pie 142
Mixed Duchess Potatoes 87
Moussaka 50
Mushroom Cheese Braids 96

N

New Potato Treat 64
Noisettes 91

O

Orange Chocolate Cake 140
Oven Fries 117
Oven Potatoes Lyonnaise 67

P

Parmesan Duchess Potatoes . . . 87
Parmesan Hash Browns 103
Parmesan Sauce 43
Patties
   Fish Cakes 60
   Latkes 82
   Potato Parcels 95
   Rum-Sauced 128
   Speedy Potato 105
   Sweet Potato 128
   Twice-Cooked Potatoes 93
Peach Sweet Potatoes 131
Perogies 84
Pies, Savory
   Chicken Pot 47
   Shepherd's 49
   Shrimp Pot 59
Pies, Sweet
   Mince 142
   Sweet Potato 147
Pinwheels 141
Pizza Hash Brown 56
Potato And Cheese Filling 84
Potato And Onion Filling. 84
Potato Appetizer Puffs 13
Potato Biscuits 20
Potato Bread 26
Potato Broccoli Soup 29
Potato Buns 27
Potato Cake 94
Potato Cheese Frittata 74
Potato Croquettes 92
Potato Crunchies 118
Potato Dumplings 79
Potato Frittata 74
Potato Heaps 102
Potato Hotcakes 23
Potato Lyonnaise. 88
Potato Mushroom Bake 66
Potato Parcels 95
Potato Parmesan Roast 116
Potato Puff Balls 100
Potato Puff Casserole 112
Potato Quiche 76
Potato Re-Run 138

Potato Salad 42
Potato Salads
   Baked 38
   Dilly 41
   German 39
   Layered 40
   Southern 37
Potato Sausage Soup 32
Potato Soufflé 77
Potato Stir-Fry 81
Potato Stuffing 61
Potato Tray Buns 27
Potato Wheat Biscuits 19
Potatoes Anna 100
Potatoes Bolognese 46
Potatoes Dauphine 86
Potatoes Dauphine Parmesan . . 86
Potatoes O'Brien 80
Potatoes Parmesan 70
Potatoes With Mushrooms . . . 114
Poutine 132

Q

Quick Cheese Potatoes 119
Quick Scallop Bake 73
Quickest Potato Biscuits 20

R

Reuben-Stuffed Potatoes 122
Roasted
   Gold Roast Potatoes 117
   Italian Potato Roast 119
   Potato Parmesan Roast . . . 116
Rum-Sauced Patties 128

S

Salads
   Baked Potato 38
   Dilly Potato 41
   German Potato 39
   Layered Potato 40
   Potato 42
   Southern Potato 37
Samosas 15
Sausage Frittata 75
Savory New Potatoes 63
Savory Potato Soup 30
Scalloped Potatoes 69
Seafood Delight 58
Sesame Sticks 14
Shepherd's Pie 49
Shrimp Pot Pie 59
Side Dishes, see pages 61-138
Soups
   Asparagus Chowder 33
   Celery Cream 31
   Cullen Skink 32
   Mashed Potato 34
   Potato Broccoli 29
   Potato Sausage 32
   Savory Potato 30
   Vichyssoise 30
Sour Cream-Stuffed Potatoes . . 122
Sour Potatoes 136
Southern Potato Salad 37
Spanish Omelet 76
Speedy Cheesy Potatoes 104

Speedy Potato Patties 105
Spudonion Pizza 57
Steamed Pudding 150
Stuffed
   Bacon And Cheese Spuds . . . 124
   Broccoli 121
   Cheese 120
   Full O' Beans Spud 120
   Kids' Stuffed Spuds 123
   Reuben 122
   Sour Cream 122
Stuffed Green Peppers 99
Sugared Doughnuts 28
Super Creamed Potatoes 136
Sweet Potato Bake 127
Sweet Potato Balls 12
Sweet Potato Cheesecake . . . 148
Sweet Potato Dessert 149
Sweet Potato Dumplings 48
Sweet Potato Loaf 25
Sweet Potato Patties 128
Sweet Potato Pie 147
Sweet Potatoes
   Apple Sweet Potato Bake . . . 133
   Apricot 131
   Candied 130
   Cranberry 130
   Dumpling Casserole 48
   Peach 131
   Rum-Sauced Patties 128

T

Tater-Topped Beef Bake 45
Thin Crust 57
Tiny Herb Garlic Spuds 64
Tomato Potato Casserole 66
Tourtière Turnovers 51
Twice-Cooked Potatoes 93

V

Vegetable Squares 12
Vegetables In Shells 98
Veggie Fritters 11
Vichyssoise 30

Y

Yams
   Apple 129
   Cranberry Hasselback 129
   Hawaiian 129

Photo Index

A
Apple Sweet Potato Bake 36
Apricot Sweet Potatoes. . . . . Front Cover
Asparagus Chowder . . . . 143, Back Cover

B
Bacon and Cheese Spuds. 125
Broccoli-Stuffed Potatoes . . . . Front Cover
Brown Grain Bread 17

C
Chocolate Cake with Chocolate Icing 144
Chocolate Cookies. 144
Cinnamon Buns. 18
Con Queso Potatoes 72
Cranberry Hasselback Yams 125
Cranberry Sweet Potatoes 35
Creamy Spinach Potatoes. 126

D
Drop Cookies 144
Duchess Potatoes. . . . . Front Cover
Dumpling Casserole. 36

G
German Potato Salad. 89
Grated Potato Rösti 89

H
Heaven And Earth 108

I
Italian Potato Roast 108

J
Jalapeño Potatoes 72

L
Latkes. 89
Layered Potato Salad . . . . Front Cover

M
Meaty Roulade 35
Moussaka 54
Mushroom Cheese Braids. 71

N
Noisettes. 107

P
Pinwheels 144
Potato Broccoli Soup 17
Potato Buns. 54
Potato Cake 53
Potato Croquettes 90
Potato Wheat Biscuits . . . . 143, Back Cover
Potatoes O'Brien 107

R
Reuben-Stuffed Potatoes 125
Rum-Sauced Patties 126

S
Savory Potato Soup 17
Sesame Sticks . . . . 143, Back Cover
Spanish Omelet. 18
Speedy Potato Patties 90
Spudonion Pizza 71
Stuffed Green Peppers 90
Sweet Potato Balls 35

T
Tiny Herb Garlic Spuds. . . . . Front Cover
Tomato Potato Casserole 54
Tourtière Turnovers 53

V
Vegetables In Shells . . . . Front Cover

155

Tip Index

B
Baked - reheating 26, 38
Boil
   perogies 85
   preboiling baked potatoes 150
   preventing curdled scalloped potatoes . . 148
   preventing darkening 46

C
Capsaicin - in jalapeños. 65
Chili - stretching a recipe 31
Cream of tartar - to prevent darkening 46
Curdling - prevention in scalloped potatoes . 148

D
Darkening
   growth in center 116
   prevention when cooking 46

F
French fries
   crispier 59
   reheating 26, 38

J
Jalapeños - wearing gloves while handling . . 65

L
Latkes - lower fat 83
Leftover potatoes - in bread 21
Lemon juice - to prevent darkening 46
Low-fat - latkes 83

M
Mashed potatoes
   fluffier 135
   reheating 26, 38
   stretching 87
Microwave
   how to cook a potato 75
   quick cook for recipes 75

N
Non-stick pans - cooking latkes 83

P
Patties - reheating 26, 38
Peeling
   after cooking 46
   after microwaving 75
   deep-frying 103
Perogies
   boiling 85
   frozen and reheated 85
   frying 85
   microwaving 85
Potato flakes - stretching mashed potatoes . . . 87
Potato liquid - in bread 21

R
Reheating
   baked 26, 38
   fries 26, 38
   mashed 26, 38
   patties 26, 38
   perogies 85
   raw, in soups or stews 26
   stuffed 26, 38

S
Scalloped potatoes - preventing curdling . . . 148
Soup - stretching a recipe 31
Stuffed - reheating 26, 38
Substitutions
   milk or water for reserved potato liquid . . 21
   skim milk powder for milk 135

U
Unexpected company
   stretching chili 31
   stretching mashed potatoes 87
   stretching soup 31

V
Vinegar - to prevent darkening 46

W
Warming potatoes - in oven 38

Feature Recipe from
Chocolate Everything

No food stimulates our senses so completely. No flavor evokes such a feeling of joy and abandon. No texture is so smooth and refined as chocolate...if not an addiction, then certainly a passion!

Mini Chip Cheesecakes

Smooth and creamy with lots of little chocolate bits. Garnish with whipped topping and Chocolate Filigrees, page 24, just before serving.

Chocolate wafers	12	12
Light cream cheese (8 oz., 250 g, each), softened	2	2
Granulated sugar	¾ cup	175 mL
Large eggs	2	2
Vanilla	1 tsp.	5 mL
Mini semisweet chocolate chips	½ cup	125 mL
Mini semisweet chocolate chips	½ cup	125 mL

Line ungreased muffin cups with large paper liners. Place 1 wafer in bottom of each liner.

Beat cream cheese and sugar in medium bowl until smooth. Beat in eggs, 1 at a time, on low just until blended. Add vanilla. Mix in.

Melt first amount of chocolate chips in small saucepan over hot water, or on low, stirring constantly, until smooth. Do not overheat. Add to batter.

Add second amount of chocolate chips. Fold in. Divide over wafers. Bake in 325°F (160°C) oven for 25 to 30 minutes until set. Cool, then chill. Makes 12.

1 cheesecake: 275 Calories; 7 g Protein; 15.2 g Total Fat; 31 g Carbohydrate; 462 mg Sodium; 1 g Dietary Fiber

Company's Coming cookbooks are available at retail locations **throughout** Canada!

See mail order form

Buy any 2 cookbooks—choose a 3rd FREE of equal or less value than the lowest price paid.   *Available in French

Original Series — CA$14.99 Canada — US$10.99 USA & International

CODE		CODE		CODE	
SQ	150 Delicious Squares*	FS	Fish & Seafood*	PA	Pasta*
AP	Appetizers	HE	Holiday Entertaining*	PI	Pies*
BA	Barbecues*	KC	Kids Cooking*	PZ	Pizza!*
BR	Breads*	LCA	Light Casseroles*	PR	Preserves*
BB	Breakfasts & Brunches*	LR	Light Recipes*	SA	Salads*
CK	Cakes	LU	Lunches*	SC	Slow Cooker Recipes*
CA	Casseroles*	MC	Main Courses	SS	Soups & Sandwiches
CH	Chicken, Etc.*	MAM	Make-Ahead Meals*	ST	Starters*
CO	Cookies*	ME	Meatless Cooking*	SF	Stir-Fry*
CT	Cooking For Two*	MI	Microwave Cooking*	PB	The Potato Book* NEW
DE	Desserts	MU	Muffins & More*	VE	Vegetables
DI	Dinners of the World	ODM	One-Dish Meals*		

Greatest Hits — CA$12.99 Canada — US$9.99 USA & International

CODE		CODE	
BML	Biscuits, Muffins & Loaves*	SAW	Sandwiches & Wraps*
DSD	Dips, Spreads & Dressings*	SAS	Soups & Salads*

Lifestyle Series — CA$16.99 Canada — US$12.99 USA & International

CODE		CODE		CODE	
GR	Grilling*	LFC	Low-fat Cooking*	LFP	Low-fat Pasta*

Special Occasion Series — CA$19.99 Canada

CODE			
CE	Chocolate Everything* NEW (Oct/00)		US$19.99 USA & International
EE	Easy Entertaining* (hardcover)		US$19.99 USA & International

Assorted Titles

CODE		
BE	Beef Today! (softcover)	CA$19.99 Canada US$15.99 USA & International

COOKBOOKS

www.companyscoming.com
visit our web-site

COMPANY'S COMING PUBLISHING LIMITED
2311 - 96 Street
Edmonton, Alberta, Canada T6N 1G3
Tel: (780) 450-6223 Fax: (780) 450-1857

Exclusive Mail Order Offer

Buy 2 Get 1 FREE!
Buy any 2 cookbooks—choose a **3rd FREE** of equal or less value than the lowest price paid.

See page 158 for list of cookbooks

Quantity	Code	Title	Price Each	Price Total
			$	$
		don't forget		
		to indicate your		
		free book(s).		
		(see exclusive mail order		
		offer above)		
		please print		
	TOTAL BOOKS (including FREE)	TOTAL BOOKS PURCHASED:	$	

	International	Canada & USA
Plus Shipping & Handling (per destination)	$7.00 (one book)	$5.00 (1-3 books)
Additional Books (including FREE books)	$ ($2.00 each)	$ ($1.00 each)
Sub-Total	$	$
Canadian residents add G.S.T (7%)		$
TOTAL AMOUNT ENCLOSED	$	$

The Fine Print

- Orders outside Canada must be **PAID IN US FUNDS** by cheque or money order drawn on Canadian or US bank or by credit card.
- Make cheque or money order payable to: **COMPANY'S COMING PUBLISHING LIMITED**.
- Prices are expressed in Canadian dollars for Canada, US dollars for USA & International and are subject to change without prior notice.
- Orders are shipped surface mail. For courier rates, visit our web-site: www.companyscoming.com or contact us: Tel: (780) 450-6223 Fax: (780) 450-1857.
- Sorry, no C.O.D's.

Gift Giving

- Let us help you with your gift giving!
- We will send cookbooks directly to the recipients of your choice if you give us their names and addresses.
- Please specify the titles you wish to send to each person.
- If you would like to include your personal note or card, we will be pleased to enclose it with your gift order.
- Company's Coming Cookbooks make excellent gifts: Birthdays, bridal showers, Mother's Day, Father's Day, graduation or any occasion...collect them all!

☐ MasterCard ☐ VISA

_____ Expiry date

Account # _____

Name of cardholder _____

Cardholder's signature _____

Shipping Address
Send the cookbooks listed above to:

Name: _____

Street: _____

City: _____ Prov./State: _____

Country: _____ Postal Code/Zip: _____

Tel: (_____) _____

E-mail address: _____

YES! Please send a catalogue: ☐ English ☐ French

Please mail or fax to:
Company's Coming Publishing Limited
2311 - 96 Street
Edmonton, Alberta, Canada   T6N 1G3
Fax: (780) 450-1857

Name:_____
Address:_____
_____
e-mail:_____

Reader Survey

We welcome your comments and would love to hear from you.
Please take a few moments to give us your feedback.

1. *Approximately what percentage of the cooking do you do in your home?* _____ %

2. *How many meals do you cook in your home in a typical week?* _____

3. *How often do you refer to a cookbook (or other source) for recipes?*
   - ❏ Everyday
   - ❏ A few times a week
   - ❏ 2 or 3 times a month
   - ❏ Once a month
   - ❏ A few times a year
   - ❏ Never

4. *What recipe features are most important to you? Rank 1 to 7;*
   (1 being most important, 7 being least important).
   - ____ Recipes for everyday cooking
   - ____ Recipes for guests and entertaining
   - ____ Easy recipes; quick to prepare, with everyday ingredients
   - ____ Low-fat or health-conscious recipes
   - ____ Recipes you can trust to work
   - ____ Recipes using exotic ingredients
   - ____ Recipes using fresh ingredients only

5. *What cookbook features are most important to you? Rank 1 to 6;*
   (1 being most important, 6 being least important).
   - ____ Lots of color photographs of recipes
   - ____ "How-to" instructions or photos
   - ____ Helpful hints & cooking tips
   - ____ Lay-flat binding (coil or plastic comb)
   - ____ Well organized with complete index
   - ____ Priced low

6. *How many cookbooks have you purchased in the last year?*

7. *Of these, how many were gifts?* _____   _____

8. *Age group*
   - ❏ Under 18
   - ❏ 18 to 24
   - ❏ 25 to 34
   - ❏ 35 to 44
   - ❏ 45 to 54
   - ❏ 55 to 64
   - ❏ 65+

9. *What do you like best about Company's Coming Cookbooks?*
   _____
   _____

10. *How could Company's Coming Cookbooks be improved?*
    _____
    _____

11. *Topics you would like to see published by Company's Coming:*
    _____
    _____

Thank you for sharing your views. We truly value your input.